SELF-ESTEEM

Respecting and Valuing Ourselves

CAROL ROGNE

outskirtspress
DENVER, COLORADO

The opinions expressed in this manuscript are solely the opinions of the author and do not represent the opinions or thoughts of the publisher. The author has represented and warranted full ownership and/or legal right to publish all the materials in this book.

Self-Esteem
Respecting and Valuing Ourselves
All Rights Reserved.
Copyright © 2012 Carol Rogne
V3.0

Cover Photo © 2012 JupiterImages Corporation. All rights reserved - used with permission.

This book may not be reproduced, transmitted, or stored in whole or in part by any means, including graphic, electronic, or mechanical without the express written consent of the publisher except in the case of brief quotations embodied in critical articles and reviews.

Outskirts Press, Inc.
http://www.outskirtspress.com

ISBN: 978-1-4327-9401-9

Outskirts Press and the "OP" logo are trademarks belonging to Outskirts Press, Inc.

PRINTED IN THE UNITED STATES OF AMERICA

Table of Contents

Acknowledgments vii
Introduction ix

Chapter 1 1
   Self-Esteem Influences All Areas of Our Life
Chapter 2 14
   Major Causes of Low Self-Esteem
- Harmful experiences in childhood diminish self-esteem 15
- Being controlled by a person or group diminishes self-esteem 20

Chapter 3 34
   Challenges to Women and Minority Persons' Self-Esteem
- The experience of having less personal power 35
- Toxic relationships 41
- Occupational power differences 43
- Religious teachings 46
- Irrational guilt 46

Chapter 4 49
   The Journey of Recovery and Personal Growth
Chapter 5 59
   Healing from Harmful Experiences in Childhood
Chapter 6 70
   Removing Self-Created Hindrances to Self-Esteem
- Recovering from addictions and addictive activities . 71
- Revising negative learning about ourselves 76
- Changing faulty thinking and negative self-talk 78
- Discarding irrational beliefs and toxic guilt 85

Chapter 7 96
  Empowerment Strategies
  - Empowering strategies when we are controlled 97
  - Empowering ourselves by meeting our emotional needs 123
  - Empowering ourselves if we are struggling with depression 124
  - Empowering ourselves by recovering from co-dependency 126
  - Empowering ourselves by thinking positively 128

Chapter 8 131
  Reflecting, Processing, and Discovering Ourselves
  - Create a lifeline 131
  - Raise your awareness by journaling 134
  - Acknowledge your strengths 135
  - Be proud of your emotional achievements 136
  - Acknowledge and work with your anger 137
  - Reflect on your relationships 143
  - Make amends and forgive yourself 145
  - Write about what you like about yourself 146
  - Relish compliments that you receive 146
  - Reflect on your miraculous body and mind 147
  - Act out emotions with body movement 149
  - Describe yourself 150
  - Feel emotionally powerful, capable, and resilient 151
  - Set goals for yourself 152
  - Use your mind to visualize 152
  - Look within for happiness 153
  - Think about joyful experiences 154
  - Write your own personal affirmations 155
  - Create a list of reasons to be grateful 157
  - Discover healthy ways to share yourself 157

Chapter 9 159
   Respecting and Valuing Ourselves
      Trusting and living our inner truth 160
      Mentally, physically, emotionally and spiritually
      nurturing ourselves 161
      Acknowledging our giftedness 162
      Identifying our goals and activating 163
      Living one day at a time 164
      Becoming energy-efficient 165
      Thinking and living creatively 166
      Standing up for what we believe 167
      Being in harmony with universal laws 168
      Connecting with people and activities
      that are positive and stimulating 169
      Laughing often 170
      Treating ourselves like our own best friend 170
      Being open to the many forms of healing 171
      Taking time for solitude 173
      Discovering and following our passion 174
      Going beyond what society considers to be normal 175
      Actualizing our potential 176
      Living with peace of mind 177
      Living each day in gratitude 179
Chapter 10 180
   Living and Sharing Our Healthy Self-Esteem
Chapter 11 195
   Achieving Emotional Balance
Chapter 12 202
   Visualizations, Affirmations, and Expressions of Gratitude

Epilogue 215
References 217

Acknowledgments

I am very grateful for my family, friends, colleagues, mentors, students, clients, and workshop participants, for sharing a part of their life journey with me. To each one of you, I send positive thoughts and prayers for your health, happiness, and self-fulfillment. Let us all respect and value ourselves, and discover that we are lovable, capable, and one of God's miracles. We will then view others and treat them in the same way. This is a first step in creating peace in our homes and peace in our world.

Introduction

Self-esteem is an indicator of our overall emotional health. Healthy, authentic self-esteem sets the stage for creating a life that accepts and overcomes challenges, is purposeful, and is enriched by relationships. This book offers a recovery and empowerment process for low self-esteem which has been life-changing for clients and students I have worked with for the past several years as a therapist.

Many books make it seem like a self-esteem healing journey can be accomplished within a few days, but this will not result in true recovery. The research regarding self-esteem is included in some books, which is important, but what most of us are looking for is a *workable recovery process*. Other books written about self-esteem make recovery from low self-esteem seem so complex and difficult that one becomes exhausted at the thought of even trying. However, recovering from low self-esteem is possible, just as lives devastated by addictions change dramatically by committing to go to any lengths to recover, which, for addictions, includes following the steps of the Twelve-Step Program. Similar to addictions, low self-esteem is serious and adversely affects our life experience, but with a commitment to our own emotional health, recovery is possible.

Low self-esteem is not our fault, but it is our struggle. We have to focus on ourselves, work through harmful childhood experiences, discard false information we learned, and empower ourselves. As we recover from low self-esteem, we will increasingly respect and value ourselves. We will become fully aware that the truth of our being is that we are *lovable and capable and one of God's miracles!*

Chapter 1

Self-Esteem Influences All Areas of Our Life

Life isn't about finding yourself. Life is about creating yourself.
—George Bernard Shaw, Irish playwright

Healthy, authentic self-esteem is a key factor in emotional, mental, physical, and spiritual health. Self-esteem not only involves feeling good about ourselves, but also feeling competent and believing that we can think clearly, manage our lives, and make choices that are life-fostering. When we have authentic self-esteem, we feel secure within ourselves, take responsibility for our lives, and live up to the expectations that we have of ourselves. We love and approve of ourselves and feel worthy. There is a sense of individuality as well as valuing emotional bonding with others. When we have healthy self-esteem, we are more likely to have positive behaviors, which, in turn, increase our level of self-esteem. Authentic self-esteem provides us with a sense of significance, which contributes to being able to create a life that is creative and purposeful. We are able to respect and value ourselves.

The dictionary defines these terms as:

Respect: *esteem for or a sense of worth or excellence of a person, a personal quality or ability*

Value: *Worth in usefulness or importance, to regard highly*

Growing in healthy self-esteem is a journey that leads to the discovery that our innate essence is worthy and valuable. Our value as a person is not about our *doing*, as society would have us believe. We do not have to achieve more to have healthy self-esteem. Rather, when we have healthy self-esteem, we will naturally achieve more in ways that bring meaning to our lives. When we have a life purpose and our actions are in alignment with what gives our life meaning, we foster and nurture our own self-esteem.

Self-esteem is not a pressing issue if we are struggling with providing ourselves and our families with the basic needs in life. However, in our society, many people have adequate food, safety, and shelter. When we have these basic needs met, we emotionally move on to addressing our self-esteem, being authentic, living our life with integrity, and becoming all that we are meant to become.

Self-esteem is often misunderstood

Self-esteem is an indicator of our emotional health. As with physical health, our lives are more apt to flourish when we have a healthy emotional life. The misunderstanding regarding self-esteem is that people with self-esteem are grandiose and have an exaggerated sense of self-importance. The truth is that authentic self-esteem is not ego-driven. Being egotistical, boastful, and self-centered are behaviors that are often a result of *low self-esteem* and personal insecurity. Persons with high self-esteem have no need to brag or show off. They are comfortable with who they are, what they are achieving, and how they are living their lives. Rather than trying to control others, they are usually cooperative and supportive to others. Contrary to what some people believe, having low self-esteem is not being modest or virtuous. Rather, it is being disrespectful of ourselves. Having respect and esteem for oneself is necessary for creating a meaningful life.

Self-esteem is not *all or nothing*

No one has 100% self-esteem all of the time, and we would like to believe that there are no people with *no* self-esteem. Self-esteem is not *all or nothing*; it is more accurately described as *more or less*. We can mentally place ourselves on a continuum from one (1) to ten (10), based on how we feel about ourselves the majority of time, in most of our adult roles. We are likely to be lower on this continuum when we experience real or perceived failure. Personal accomplishments usually result in temporarily feeling good about ourselves, and we place ourselves higher on the continuum. However, to have a *daily sense of being worthy*, many of us have to consciously choose to raise our level of self-esteem by starting a process of changing our thoughts, attitudes, beliefs, and behaviors.

Self-esteem has ups and downs based on life experiences

Though we may have healthy self-esteem, there are times when we are overwhelmed with challenges, we do not feel very competent or confident, or we make choices and behave in ways that are disappointing to ourselves. Experiences that are likely to cause our self-esteem to diminish include divorce, the loss of a job, any type of rejection, reprimands, or behaving in ways that cause harm to others. We emotionally recover our usual level of self-esteem within a period of time, especially if we can correct the problem, unless the experience is traumatic and creates emotional and personal devastation.

Relationships also have a profound effect on our self-esteem. Our self-esteem is lowered when someone is routinely controlling and being disrespectful to us. A quick measure regarding the health of a relationship is to recall our level of self-esteem when we entered the relationship, and how we currently view our self-esteem. If our level of self-esteem is much lower than before we became involved with the other person, we are in an unhealthy relationship.

Self-esteem may be different in various situations

We function in different roles, such as being a parent, spouse, employee, employer, friend, or colleague. We may feel competent and confident in our occupational roles, but feel inadequate when relating to a partner, participating in social events, or when parenting children. Though it is not apparent to others, we may struggle with low self-esteem and lack self-confidence in particular situations, in some areas of our work, or with certain people.

Self-esteem is our emotional root system

The roots of plants, though unseen, need nutrients, sunshine, and moisture to survive. Healthy roots are necessary for healthy plants. Self-esteem is our root system and determines our level of emotional health. Humans, like the roots of plants, need nutrients and sunshine to grow in healthy ways. It doesn't work to do things like buying a new outfit or electronic device, or using alcohol or drugs. Though we may think that certain activities and chemicals help us to feel better, they are temporary highs and do not foster authentic and healthy self-esteem.

Our emotional root system determines the quality of our lives. If we ignore our roots, we will not experience mental, emotional, physical, and spiritual well-being. Therefore, it is important to discover the true nutrients that nourish our roots, such as respecting, valuing, loving, honoring, accepting, embracing, and appreciating ourselves. When provided with these nutrients, our roots, our relationships, and our lives flourish. Unless we experience hindrances that are out of our control, we will readily meet life's challenges and function well throughout our lives.

Self-esteem, together with other factors such as physical health and intelligence, affects all areas of our life. If these factors are compromised, our life is likely to be more difficult and less fulfilling. However, we know of people who rise above their disabilities and create a purposeful and meaningful life. In contrast are those people who are loved by their family members, friends, and colleagues but do not love themselves. They can be admired but regard themselves as unworthy. They may present themselves as competent but feel incompetent. They can be given awards, but do not savor their success because they feel like they have done nothing out of the ordinary, or they attribute their success to luck. We have all read about some superstars and high-profile people who appear to have it all, but they are neither happy nor peaceful within themselves.

Healthy self-esteem influences our:

- Relationship we have with ourselves
- Relationships with others
- Ability to respond to the challenge of change
- Expectations of success
- Willingness to share thoughts, ideas, and feelings
- Level of trust in our intuitions, perceptions, and decisions
- Ability to deal with loss
- Emotional, physical, mental, and spiritual health

Self-esteem affects the relationship we have with *ourselves*

Our level of self-esteem affects how we feel about ourselves, how we relate to ourselves, and how we nurture ourselves. Persons with high self-esteem have usually taken time to become better acquainted with themselves and accept both their strong and weak areas. When a person with high self-esteem experiences frustration, criticism, or failure, they feel discouraged like anyone else, but they are more resilient and are able to return to their normal thoughts, emotions, and activities in a shorter period of time. They learn from past mistakes, strive to change thoughts and behaviors that are self-sabotaging, and move forward with their lives. People with high self-esteem are friendly toward themselves and enjoy being alone at times. Their inner dialogue is usually positive, and they are excited about their lives because they are moving toward their goals and becoming the person they are meant to be. Persons with authentic self-esteem are enthusiastic about life and strive to be their best self, which requires living by their highest ethical and spiritual principles.

In contrast, persons with low self-esteem are often harsh and negative with themselves, and their inner self-talk is often self-berating. The feelings of being inferior, unworthy, and having less value than others take center stage in their emotional life. They have a low level of self-acceptance and do not acknowledge, or minimize, their skills and talents. Persons with low self-esteem can quickly generate a list of negative traits about themselves but are often uncomfortable or unable to list their good qualities. Their relationship with themselves is neither comfortable nor peaceful, and too often they would prefer to be someone else. Rather than being their own best friend, people who struggle with low self-esteem are often their own worst enemy, having attitudes and behaviors that block emotional and personal growth. Low self-esteem often contributes to low achievement, wasted human potential, and dissatisfaction with life. Emotional, physical, and spiritual health is adversely affected.

Self-esteem affects relationships with *others*

Persons with high self-esteem care about themselves and, therefore, are able to care about others in healthy ways. The caring they extend to others is by *choice*, rather than being driven by false guilt, sacrificing oneself, or needing to control. Though they are not immune from unhealthy relationships, they are less likely to sabotage relationships by their dysfunctional behaviors.

Persons with low self-esteem experience more turmoil, anger, and stress in relationships, often blaming others for their difficulties rather than taking personal responsibility. They may try to control others or engage in manipulative mind games to be the center of attention and have all of their desires met. Some people with low self-esteem are shy, withdrawn, and fearful when relating to others, whereas others are arrogant, rude, critical of others, and put on a false front of being superior. Unable to meet many of their own needs, they often place unrealistic expectations on spouses, children, or friends. Frequently, low self-esteem people feel powerless and that they are victims of others' unkindness or insensitivity. When their thoughts, ideas, and feelings are predominantly negative, they often experience healthy people drifting away from them.

**Self-esteem influences the willingness
to share thoughts, ideas, and feelings**

High self-esteem people readily share ideas and feelings with people they trust, in appropriate and meaningful ways. Rather than monopolizing conversations, they are usually good listeners and are honest in their communication. They care about others, and because they readily share feelings, emotional closeness and positive energies are generated in their relationships.

People with low self-esteem have difficulty sharing themselves with others. They may feel inferior, they may not be in touch with their feelings, or they may believe their thoughts would not be accepted by others. Also, having been taught as children by dysfunctional family members to never share family secrets, these adults often experience guilt if they talk about the problems in their family of origin or the difficulties they are having in current relationships. They often repress feelings such as anger, hurt, and resentments, which is detrimental to emotional and physical health.

**Self-esteem influences the degree to which
we trust our intuition, perceptions, and decisions**

People with high self-esteem are self-directed. Although they ask for advice when needed, they do not blindly follow the opinions of others. They view reality as it is and take responsibility for themselves, rather than distorting or denying what really is occurring. Trusting their inner truth, intuition, perceptions, and decisions, they move forward and make changes as needed.

In contrast, people with low self-esteem have difficulty trusting themselves. Second-guessing their perceptions and decisions is common, and they are likely to depend on other's advice rather than being inner-directed.

Self-esteem influences our ability to deal with loss

The emotional pain involved in personal losses is no less difficult for individuals with high self-esteem than it is for those with low self-esteem. However, those with a higher level of self-esteem are able to return to normal functioning in a shorter period of time because they have a relationship with their inner self—a reliable and trustworthy friend they can depend on when experiencing loss. They can be their own comforters, along with friends and family with whom they can share their painful feelings, which is an important part of working through grief.

Low self-esteem persons have more difficulty letting go and moving on with their lives when they experience loss. Because they may not have cultivated inner strength on which they can depend during difficult times, they are often less resilient. They may also have fewer healthy friends, fewer options if the loss is regarding work, or they may have very limited opportunities or an unwillingness to participate in activities that provide emotional renewal.

Self-esteem influences our ability to respond to the challenge of change

Change poses challenges in our life and requires openness to new learning and flexibility. A person with high self-esteem has self-confidence and the emotional stability to accept the challenge of new ideas and different perspectives. These people are able to objectively assess beliefs that are contrary to their own. Rather than succumbing to fear and putting energies into resistance, high self-esteem people trust themselves and use their emotional strength and coping skills as they move through personal transitions. People with high self-esteem will often create new challenges for themselves and often put at risk what they have previously achieved. They are less hesitant to put themselves in situations where the outcome is unknown. Persons with healthy self-esteem focus on *process* rather than on outcome and usually find positives as they venture forward, such as the benefit of new learning.

People with limited self-esteem are more inclined to prefer routine in tasks, ideas, experiences, and relationships. Change is often met with resistance because it generates emotional fear. Although this approach may feel more comfortable than facing and working through challenges, it hinders full development.

Self-esteem influences expectations of success

Individuals with high self-esteem expect success in their encounters with new people or new ventures. Though they may experience anxious moments, they spend little time thinking about how they might fail. Even if they don't experience *total* success, they appreciate the positive aspects of the experience.

In contrast, people with low self-esteem are likely to set themselves up to be unsuccessful because they focus on the negative possibilities and predict failure. They often do not see the benefits of trying new activities and mentally and emotionally stretching and growing. These individuals often internalize failure and generalize it to other parts of their lives. They also take longer to bounce back from defeat or criticism.

Self-esteem influences our emotional, physical, mental, and spiritual health

People with high self-esteem are usually emotionally balanced. They are diligent in taking care of their physical bodies, have positive self-talk, healthy relationships, are involved in meaningful activities, and have a sense of control regarding their life. All of these factors promote emotional and physical health.

People with low self-esteem often engage in negative self-talk and hold irrational beliefs, which generate stress, fear, and anxiety. There is typically less healthy mental, emotional, physical, and spiritual self-nurturing. They often feel like they have little control over their lives, which is a perception that adversely affects emotional and physical health.

There may be *unhealthy* emotional benefits for keeping our low self-esteem

Low self-esteem may carry emotional rewards that create an unwillingness to change. There is also a natural resistance to changing routines, behaviors, and attitudes, even if they are creating problems for us. Some unhealthy reasons for keeping our low self-esteem may be:

- Liking the feeling of being dependent on others to meet our emotional, social, entertainment, and physical needs
- Feeling that low self-esteem is virtuous
- Refusing to take responsibility for ourselves
- Knowing that needy, angry, or whiny people get more attention
- Being stuck in self-pity
- Feeling that change is impossible or it wouldn't make any difference
- Thinking that if we decided to be healthier, we would have to give up our addictions
- Being unwilling to lose the control we have over other persons by acting needy and helpless
- Fearing that there will be more expectations put on us if we become emotionally healthy

Established patterns, though pain-producing, are emotionally safe and secure. Change is often viewed as risky and frightening. We usually don't voluntarily choose to start making changes until we realize that changing our thoughts and actions will be less stressful, risky, and emotionally painful than continuing behaviors that are not working for us.

◄ Self-Esteem

Low self-esteem is a serious problem in our society

Though we claim to be a civilized society, we have rates of domestic violence and child abuse and neglect that are totally unacceptable and disgraceful. Every year, there are thousands of mandated reports of physical or sexual abuse filed with child protection agencies. In addition, countless numbers of children are neglected and verbally abused. One of the key factors in domestic violence and child abuse is chemical addiction, which creates a high risk for inappropriate and abusive behaviors, including harming spouses and innocent children with anger. Mental health professionals, child protection workers, parents, educators, sociologists, clergy, and other adults who interact with children are extremely concerned about our high rates of domestic violence and child abuse, which always creates emotional trauma.

As a result of adult dysfunction, far too many young people suffer from low self-esteem. Bullies, who act in grandiose and abusive ways to hide their feelings of low self-esteem and other emotional difficulties, are an increasing problem in schools and in our society. Low self-esteem is often an underlying cause for drug, alcohol, and sexual addictions, school failure, aggressiveness, psychological disorders, self-mutilation, eating disorders, teenage pregnancy, dropping out of school, gang involvement, high rates of violence, and suicide.

In our country, forty to fifty percent of marriages end in divorce, and children are the powerless victims who are expected to adjust to a biological parent no longer being in their home. Children are often faced with a new person whom they are expected to care about and view as their parent. They are directed to be friendly and cooperative with step-siblings if their mother or father's new relationship involves other children. Children's self-esteem is lowered in direct proportion to the emotional trauma they experience when their parents' divorce.

Low self-esteem is an ongoing epidemic in our culture and needs to be taken very seriously. However, our society does not prioritize taking care of our emotional, mental, and spiritual health. As a society, we seem to be more interested in activities that keep us *away* from our feelings. There are numerous best-selling murder mysteries in bookstores. There is violence on television and easy access to pornography on the Internet. Children are being mesmerized and conditioned by video games and are entertained by violence. Because we do not prioritize being emotionally healthy and are often unwilling to look at our own dysfunctional behaviors, we routinely fail to direct energies toward enhancing the self-esteem of ourselves and of our children. As a result, our societal problems continue to increase.

Self-esteem is necessary for mental and emotional health, as well as for healthy relationships. When we consider our social ills, it becomes obvious that our society needs to recognize the importance of self-esteem and ensure that every child is physically and emotionally safe and receives healthy parenting and love. There needs to be an abundance of information on self-esteem, and classes need to be made available and accessible to parents, grandparents, and anyone who is a caretaker of children. It is often stated that children are our greatest resource. We must put actions behind our words.

> **Because self-esteem is so vital to our lives, it is important to understand what self-esteem *is* and what self-esteem is *not*. Self-esteem is our emotional root system and affects all areas of our life. To create a less violent world, we need to prioritize concentrated efforts into fostering healthy self-esteem in all adults and children.**

Chapter 2

Major Causes of Low Self-Esteem

Children have more need of models than of critics.
—Carolyn Coats

    By observing the behaviors of infants and toddlers, we can conclude that children are born with healthy self-esteem. Infants and toddlers readily express their feelings, smiling and laughing when happy and crying when they are distraught or uncomfortable. Before they acquire language, they communicate by a variety of sounds and body language and are persistent in their efforts to be understood. When they fall down when learning to walk, they keep on trying until they are successful at not only walking, but running. They learn from anything that is presented to them, with all of their senses. Very young children do not scold themselves when they spill their food or eat with their fingers before they are able to handle utensils. They don't try to be invisible because they feel that there is something wrong with them, such as being slow in learning or clumsy. Infants and toddlers are creative, imaginative, and joyful. They are content when their needs are met. Before they understand words, they know the people they can trust to keep them safe, nurture, and love them. All of these characteristics of normal, healthy infants and toddlers indicate a high level of self-esteem.

If we had authentic self-esteem as infants and toddlers, we are apt to question when and why our self-esteem was diminished or lost. There are many causes of low self-esteem that are addressed in this book, but perhaps the two that are the most detrimental are:

- ❖ Harmful experiences in childhood
- ❖ Being controlled by a person or group

Harmful experiences in childhood diminish self-esteem

We started interacting with people from the day we were born. The people in our environment involved parents, grandparents, and siblings in the early months of life, and then expanded to extended family, friends of the family, school, and community. Any type of physical, sexual, or verbal abuse creates deep emotional, mental, and physical wounding. Adults are three or four times larger than a child, a fact that creates fear and panic when harsh, scolding, and shaming words are spoken. When children are traumatized, emotional growth is arrested. Abused children carry their emotional pain into their adulthood and struggle with more emotional, mental, relationship, and physical problems.

Most of us were not physically or emotionally abused. But we may have had parents who lacked parenting skills, loved us but never told us, or acted in ways that communicated to us that we weren't living up to their expectations, so did not deserve to be loved. We may have felt abandoned because our parents were gone, or when they were with us, they were distracted and did not listen or interact with us. Some of us were criticized more than we were affirmed, and we frequently heard statements that were shaming, negative, and hurtful. We may have had parents who passed on their emotional issues onto us, including low self-esteem. Too often, we may have been told that our behavior was bad, although our behavior may have been age-appropriate or triggered by adults' dysfunctional behaviors. Our conclusion may have been that we were not important, that we made too many mistakes, and that we were not loved because there was something innately wrong with us.

Parents usually parent their children similar to how they were parented. Adults often do not realize that parenting requires a variety of skills, nor do they fully realize that children learn from watching parents' and other people's behaviors. If parents handle conflicts with aggressive words or behaviors, children learn to do the same. When parents are dishonest and manipulative, children are likely to behave in the same manner. If parents relieve stress and frustrations with alcohol or drugs, children often do the same when they are older. Family dynamics are also adversely affected by such uncontrollable factors as emotional or mental disorders, sickness, death, the handicap of a family member, poverty, or lack of employment, which causes financial stress.

When parenting is viewed as controlling, corrective, and competitive, rather than a teaching and encouraging process, the focus narrows to what children are doing wrong, rather than what they are doing right. This results in too few affirmations and too many criticisms. Focusing on negative behaviors creates havoc with children's self-esteem and also reinforces the behavior. When attention is given to misbehavior rather than to positive behaviors, the negative behaviors are likely to be repeated.

Controlling parents often devalue their children's thoughts, ideas, projects, conversations, athletic performance, intelligence, academic grades, body size, interests, and feelings. They are determined to win power struggles with children, often over trivial issues. When parents are controlling and highly critical, children feel powerless. They often harbor anger and resentments and are likely to rebel when they are older and stronger.

Many parents do not separate personhood from behaviors when they discipline children. Children routinely hear statements that communicate that they are bad or inadequate. In contrast, when behaviors are viewed separately, children are viewed as *good* people who sometimes make poor choices and behave in negative ways, but bad choices do not make them bad persons. Children do not improve their behavior by being told that they are bad.

Children are usually not able to distinguish between healthy or unhealthy communication or true or false information. Children view parents as powerful, strong, and right. When there are problems, they feel at fault. They seldom understand that parents may lack parenting skills, make mistakes, and behave in inappropriate ways.

Children's self-esteem is dramatically diminished when adults:

- Are physically, sexually, emotionally, and verbally abusive
- Aggressively express their anger using harsh words and profanity
- Make demands and warnings in loud voices
- Are sarcastic and demeaning
- Communicate in ways that make children feel guilty or inadequate
- Blame children for things that go wrong in the family
- Have unrealistic expectations and become angry when they are not met
- Are dishonest
- Break promises
- Manipulate children against the other parent with false or distorted information
- Have an attitude of entitlement and treat children like possessions
- Frequently point out faults, but seldom give affirmations

◄ Self-Esteem

The underlying message to children in many dysfunctional families is "You are inadequate," which is communicated by statements such as:

- You can't do anything right.
- You shouldn't think that way.
- You shouldn't feel that way.
- You are driving me crazy!
- You are not good at sports…school…other activities
- If you really loved me, you would…
- See? I told you so!
- You should know better!
- Your room is always messy!
- You should be more grateful!
- Hurry up! You are so slow!
- You are so selfish!
- When are you ever going to start thinking straight?
- Sarcastically spoken, "Oh, you poor child. Your feelings got hurt."
- Don't bother me.
- Don't feel special.

There are also toxic and confusing statements spoken to children, but the *underlying* message or actual behaviors are different:

✓ I love you	…but go away.
✓ You can't do anything right	…but I need you to do something.
✓ Always tell the truth	…but when you tell the truth, I'll get angry.
✓ I'll always be there for you	…I promise I'll be there *next* time.

- ✓ I want to hear what you say   ...but I'm too busy to listen.
- ✓ You are important to me   ...but I don't have time for you.
- ✓ Everyone makes mistakes   ...but you shouldn't make mistakes.

These types of mixed-message statements make children feel like they can do nothing right. As a result, children's self-esteem is diminished, which contributes to poor achievement, lack of self-confidence, misbehaviors, and routinely making poor choices.

What we learn about ourselves in childhood will be the basis for our beliefs about ourselves in adulthood. If we were not nurtured, encouraged, and affirmed when we were young, and our mistakes and weaknesses, many of which were age-appropriate, were constantly pointed out and emphasized, we entered adulthood feeling inadequate. When we are adults, we judge ourselves based on what we learned from parents, teachers, clergy, and other significant people who interacted with us. The beliefs we have about ourselves are distorted because they are based on the false and demeaning statements that we heard from people who supposedly cared for us. This creates a high risk for *becoming* what dysfunctional people have told us we are, and we may drop out of school, have troubled relationships, abuse alcohol or drugs, be involved with law enforcement, or be unable to function independently.

- Brian talks about his childhood experiences:

    I was never really physically harmed, but I never could do anything right for my father. He would criticize me about my hair, the clothes I liked to wear, and my friends. I stopped having my buddies come over to my house because he would always make some nasty remarks about us. One day when I was a teenager, we were out in the barn doing chores and he kept criticizing and badgering me and I lost control. I hit him hard in the chest and he fell down. I left the barn, thinking that he could do the chores by himself if he couldn't shut up. Now he had something really to complain about—me not doing the chores. I couldn't wait for the next three months to pass when I could graduate and leave home. I would rather live in someone's basement or garage than live with him.

As adults, we may have less contact with our parents or other critical voices, but we became so programmed with these false messages that we keep on *telling ourselves* the same type of negative statements. We believe we are inadequate and that other people *do it better* or *are better*. We usually gravitate to people who have the same level of self-esteem. We partner with a person who shows interest and seems to care about us, and expect them to validate us, fill our emotional emptiness, and make us happy.

If we learned anything contrary to the fact that we are worthy and have value, we need to discard this false information and replace it with a belief that we are worthy and have value as created beings. Self-esteem recovery is possible, but we have to realize that our low self-esteem resulted from many harmful experiences that more than likely happened over a long period of time. A recovery process will not be instant, but we will discover that each step of the process will prove to be worth the effort.

Being controlled by a person or group diminishes self-esteem

Many of our harmful childhood experiences involved adult power used abusively. As adults, we often continue to struggle with power being used to control us in oppressive ways. Although our society is moving toward equality for all, there are still differences in power between dominant and subordinate persons and groups. The reality is far different from what was declared by our forefathers: "We hold these truths to be self-evident, that all men are created equal, that they are endowed by their Creator with certain inalienable Rights, that among these rights are Life, Liberty and the pursuit of Happiness." —United States Declaration of Independence.

Controller takes a one-up superior position

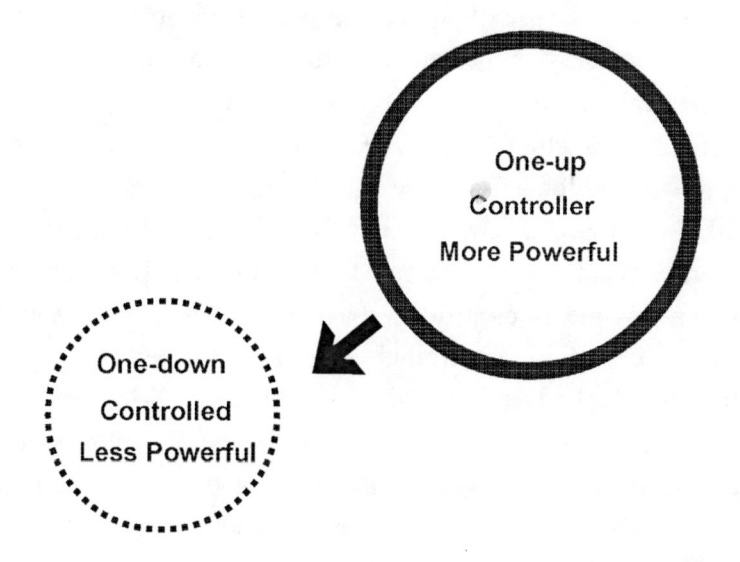

One-up
Controller
More Powerful

One-down
Controlled
Less Powerful

This diagram illustrates a more powerful person or group of persons, and a less powerful person or group of persons and describes personal relationships as well as groups within and between countries. More powerful persons who use their power to control others actually have more power or take more power in what should be an equal adult relationship. Achieving and staying in control of others involves preying on persons who are perceived and treated as weaker and have less value. Controllers, in efforts to maintain their benefits, minimize the significance of power differences as a way to prevent challenges to power inequalities. The history behind the Civil Rights Act attests to the fact that changing power inequities is very difficult and sometimes requires exceptional acts of courage and bravery to the point of risking and even losing one's life.

Power is the ability to influence others and can be used to empower others by teaching, supporting, encouraging, or providing resources. In contrast, power can be used to physically, sexually, economically, mentally, and emotionally harm others. Though silent and unseen, the positive or negative use of power affects all of us, in our personal relationships, work systems, between groups of people, and countries. When power—based on a real or perceived superior intellect, social position, physical strength, knowledge, weapons, or wealth—is used to oppress others for self-serving benefits, the power is used abusively. The abusive use of power ranges from disrespectful name-calling to violent acts that cause emotional trauma, physical harm, and death.

When anyone is controlled by a person or group, their self-esteem suffers. Being controlled by a powerful person or persons is often overlooked as being a major cause for low self-esteem. However, how power is used affects all of us. To understand ourselves, we have to be aware of the abusive use of power that we may have experienced in the past or are experiencing in current relationships. When we are controlled, not only does our self-esteem suffer, but other human rights and opportunities are diminished or removed. When we are rendered less powerful, we are placed at a disadvantage and are less likely to be able to confront the inequalities and oppression we are experiencing.

The controllers in our lives may be:

- ✓ Spouses, ex-spouses, parents, siblings, children
- ✓ In-laws, dating partners, friends, neighbors, colleagues
- ✓ Dominant groups in society

- ✓ Oppressive government, economic, religious, and political systems
- ✓ Addictions and addictive behaviors (see Chapter 6)

Dominant persons who use their power to control others have no intention of changing power inequities because they are receiving benefits from subordinate people. If extremely abusive controlling behaviors such as physical and sexual abuse, verbal expressions of rage, threats, harassment, abusive name-calling, intimidation, isolation, and humiliation are experienced, law enforcement or legal assistance needs to be accessed for protection and safety.

When dominant people use their power to control others, they often negate the feelings, thoughts, beliefs, and values of people who they perceive and treat as subordinate and who have less value. Dominant people often make decisions for subordinate people, thinking that they know what is best for them. The cycle continues when dominant people are also *given* power by less powerful people because of the fear of reprimand, consequences, or increased conflict. Women, minority persons, and other less powerful people's compliance is often mistakenly viewed as cooperation, despite the fact that the compliance is actually *forced compliance because there is a fear of consequences if one does not comply.* This is not true cooperation, which is more likely to happen within relationships where each adult has equal power.

◄ Self-Esteem

Emotional and mentally controlling behaviors lie on a continuum:

1	2	3
The controlling behaviors are often communicated through criticism, demeaning statements, and sarcasm. They are intermittent and often related to certain ongoing relationship issues.	The controlling behaviors are frequent, anger-based, critical, and sarcastic, with unpredictable causes and with unpredictable levels of intensity.	The controlling behaviors are pervasive and frightening, creating emotional fear in adults and children. There is an underlying threat that the control may escalate into physical abuse.

The emotional harm done to others is also on a continuum

1	2	3
The emotional harm causes irritation, frustration, lack of self-confidence, and diminished self-esteem.	The emotional harm causes frequent stress, anger, and low self-esteem. Beliefs, values, priorities, and freedom to develop one's life are sacrificed to prevent conflict.	The emotional harm is severe, abusive, and debilitating. People obey, comply, and often keep silent to prevent conflict and possible violence. Survival is far more crucial than self-esteem.

As the continuum on this chart indicates, the degree of control differs, and the amount of emotional damage created by the control varies as well, but all control is interpersonally violent.

Controllers are both male and female, but our society gives permission for males to be dominant and discourages the same for females. Controllers can be polite and very caring, especially in the early stages of relationships. They can also be mean, moody, and threatening to get what they want. Many emotional and mental controllers cause the greatest amount of emotional stress and devastation to their family members, who they claim to love the most.

We can easily identify the controllers in our lives by thinking about the people we would like to escape from because of feeling oppressed, obligated, or inadequate. Controllers are the people who we are tempted to be dishonest with, or we actually tell lies or make up false excuses to prevent conflict, to avoid being with them or doing something with them that we don't want to do. It is not uncommon to feel that we are being held hostage in a relationship with a controller.

Regardless of gender or group affiliation, if we are taught and treated as inferiors from an early age, self-confidence and self-esteem are lowered. Eventually, it is not only controllers who impose limitations on us. When we are socialized into thinking that we have less value, we are likely to impose *limitations on ourselves* because of being taught, accepting, and believing that we are inferior, inadequate, and incapable of designing and orchestrating our own life.

Controlling tactics assure that power structures remain unequal. Being socialized into believing that a person or group of persons are less important and have less value than more powerful people is a form of oppression. Women, members of minority groups, and people who are viewed by controllers as being *different* are more likely to experience being oppressed by more powerful people. Being controlled sets the stage for physical health problems, depression, anxiety, and being vulnerable to addictions and addictive activities. Being emotionally compromised because of their fear of controllers renders oppressed people less able to confront a more powerful person or group, which helps to fuel and maintain the existing power inequities.

When we are forced to comply with a controller's demands, we do not develop our authentic self, because our energies are used to think and behave in ways that pacify and please the controller. When we have a controller or controllers in our life, there is little time to self-reflect and embrace who we really are emotionally, mentally, and spiritually. Rather than increasingly becoming self-actualized persons, our focus and energies are directed into avoiding conflict with the controller. Our personal growth is compromised, if not arrested completely.

Historically and currently, many less powerful people are challenging the inequality among people and are leading the way to equality for less powerful people not only in our country, but around the world. However, when power inequities are challenged, there is often increased conflict and a tighter alignment of those in power. Less powerful people are discredited and punished. Many persons have experienced their lives threatened, and others have died in the struggle for equality, which indicates how important it is for powerful people to maintain their power and control.

Though we may not be experiencing extreme abuse, we may be experiencing emotional and mental abuse in a controlling relationship. Controllers' behaviors, such as being critical, taking over conversations, or ordering, directing, and commanding, are ways of taking a *one-up* position. There are only *two power positions: up or down* when one uses a competitive, dichotomous way of thinking, which is a common way that controllers think. Taking a *one-up* position is sometimes called *capping*. *One-up* comments can be about

One-up, One-down Control Maneuver

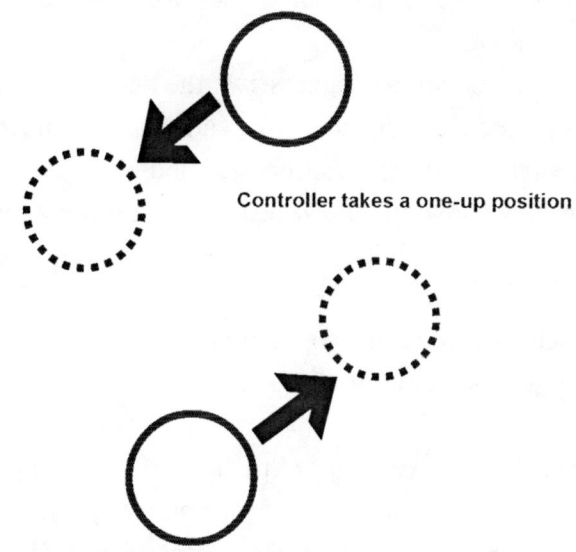

Controller takes a one-up position

Controller takes a one-down position, manupulating with guilt

trivial things, for example, "You eat weird." A typical statement that controllers communicate is "You shouldn't feel that way," which implies that if persons have hurt feelings regarding what a controller said or did, they are too sensitive and the fault is placed on them, which is a way that the controller avoids taking responsibility for the manipulative, unfair statement/s. Frequently controllers take a *one-up*, superior position by more serious personal attacks such as, "You are so screwed up, it's unbelievable!" Or, "You wouldn't last a day without me!" or, "You can't do anything right!"

In contrast, a controller might take a *one-down* position, usually *when a one-up position is not successful* at getting compliance. This is commonly known as the **guilt trip**, where the controller postures as being helpless or victimized and uses guilt in efforts to control another person. Examples of *one-down* statements are "You shouldn't expect me to do that!" Or, "You'd do anything for the kids, but you don't lift a finger for me!" The unspoken messages are that the person being manipulated does not care enough or is selfish and inconsiderate.

The *one-up* position is aggressive; the *one-down* position is passive. If we listen closely to conversations, we can identify when controllers take a *one-up* position— sounding disturbed or angry— and when they use a *one-down* position and project guilt, in efforts to have us comply with their requests.

Power used to control is often expressed through aggressive anger or guilt

Anger: Aggressive anger is perhaps the most common way of controlling others. A controller takes a *one-up* position by being aggressively angry, critical, and demanding. Controlling others with aggressive anger is interpersonally violent. **Violence is any word, look, sign, or action that hurts a person's body, possessions, dignity, or security.**

Along with being demanding, controllers are often sarcastic, which is anger expressed indirectly as a way of taking a *one-up* power position. Sarcastic individuals often have high levels of internal anger and temporarily feel better by making others feel badly by insults, threats, or disrespectful name-calling. Often, controllers claim that their sarcastic comments are *teasing*. If their victims react with anger or hurt feelings, they will say, "What's the matter? Can't you take a joke?" Or, "Don't be so sensitive. I was only kidding." By manipulating in this way, they claim innocence of any harmful actions.

When anger is expressed aggressively, combined with the power that comes with physical size, strength, and being of the male gender, it often feels like there is a potential for harm. For this very reason, people comply, agree, and enable the aggressive behaviors to avoid conflict and to protect themselves and their children. If the aggressive anger is confronted, the controller often escalates the anger, makes excuses, or blames others. Aggressive anger is efficient because people often respond quickly to demands out of fear, whereas negotiating and compromising are more time-consuming and require more communication skills. When less powerful people are fearful of the consequences of not being compliant, they lose their freedom of choice and the ability to direct their own lives, which has a negative impact on their self-esteem. (Rogne, C., 2010, *Who's Controlling You? Who Are You Controlling? – Strategies for Change.*).

- Cindy shares:

    When I look back, I can't believe all of the things I did to avoid his anger. I would try to make everything just right for him when he came home, and I tried to keep the kids quiet. Many times, he threw his supper down the sink when it wasn't something he liked or it wasn't just right. Then he would expect me to make him another supper. I would do it, so he would settle down and the kids wouldn't go to bed thinking about what happened at supper and be scared. Finally I realized that I would never please him and started planning on how I was going to leave him. I started distancing myself from him, and I know I was really cold, but that's how I felt. So that started another whole list of accusations about how bad I was, which I believed for a long time, but were never true.

Guilt: Similar to aggressive anger, guilt is a common way of controlling others, either by taking a *one-up,* aggressive stance, or a *one-down,* passive position. Controllers put others on *guilt trips* to get compliance. Controllers who take a **one-up** power position to instill guilt in others:

- ✓ Do not recognize others' personal rights, such as the right to make one's own choices
- ✓ Blame others and make false or exaggerated accusations to instill guilt
- ✓ Know that by presenting themselves as powerful and making others feel guilty, they are likely to get their requests met
- ✓ Present themselves as having the right way and others are inferior and inadequate
- ✓ Are oblivious to the resistance and obligation that controlled people feel, but usually do not express

Typical statements from an *aggressive, one-up* position intended to instill guilt in others:

You are never here when I need you.
If you really loved me, you would know what to do.
If you had a brain, this wouldn't have happened!
You have to work late…again?
We are broke again? Where are you spending all the money?
No supper made? What have you been doing all day?
I can never depend on you! You are always screwing things up!
You're going to visit your friend…again?
You are so stubborn!
You are lazy and good for nothing…a total loser!

These put-down statements are often accepted and internalized by people who respond to requests, even if they are unreasonable and controlling, because of feeling guilty.

Guilt can also be projected on others by posturing as being

helpless and weak. The controller takes a *one-down* position, acting victimized and insinuating that the other person is insensitive or uncaring. An example of a *one-down* statement is "I can't possibly pay you because I have so many other bills." The unspoken message is that the other person is insensitive because they expect to be paid by someone who is financially over-burdened and helpless to do anything about it. By taking a *one-down* position, the recipient of the guilt will often agree or comply because of feeling guilty and obligated.

Controllers who take a *helpless,* **one-down** position to instill guilt in others:

- ✓ Make others believe that they will suffer if others do not meet their demands
- ✓ Pose as helpless, innocent, and virtuous
- ✓ Imply that other people are unkind, unsympathetic, and uncaring if they do not comply with their requests
- ✓ Imply that negative consequences could happen, such as removing someone from a last will and testament; or hinting about getting sick, such as having a heart attack; or giving up on life if requests are not met with compliance

Typical statements from a *passive, one-down* position intended to instill guilt in others:

You expect me to do all that?
I haven't heard from you for so long, I thought you died.
But when you're gone, I'm all alone with nothing to do.
Don't make supper... I'll just eat a can of beans!
I am so unhappy and you seem to be happy every day!
You just don't care enough about me!

Go ahead: take the last morsel of food. I haven't eaten today but enjoy.

You're not coming home for Christmas?

I feel badly, but I know that you aren't even concerned.

You are the only person I can talk to, but you are always doing other things.

Controlling persons take advantage of nice, caring, friendly people who often act out of obligation rather than choice and who frequently compromise their physical, mental, emotional, and spiritual selves by putting aside their values, beliefs, and goals to get along with the controller. Guilt-making controllers, who are apt to be dependent and expect others to do things for them, need guilt-takers who will accept the guilt. People who are controlled by guilt often become emotionally dishonest to prevent conflicts, and say "yes" when they really want to say "no."

When controllers manipulate by using guilt, they seem to *make* us feel guilty, because we do not realize that we have a choice whether or not to feel guilty. It is important to learn that just because someone tries to put us on a guilt trip doesn't mean we have to go there, unless there is a safety concern.

- Jenny shares:

    I think guilt is my middle name. I feel guilty for not living up to my parents' expectations because they wanted me to be a teacher so I had a steady income. But that just isn't me. So I followed what I loved to do, which was being involved in theatre. I love what I do, but the income is sporadic. I suppose we all look for that one big chance to be offered a great role. It's not only my parents that make me feel guilty. My husband thinks I should be working at a steady job like he does, but I really want to be at home as much as possible with our two children. I can do that because many of my rehearsals are at night. But I understand why he feels that he supports the family far more than I do. I love acting, but I feel like I shouldn't be doing it and feel guilty a lot of the time.

> **Harmful experiences in childhood are devastating to our self-esteem, and we usually carry our emotional wounds into our adulthood. Many of these experiences involved power being used in abusive ways. We can grow in our awareness as to the harmful experiences in our childhood and ways that we are currently being controlled, which are important steps in recovering from low self-esteem.**

Chapter 3

Challenges to Women and Minority Persons' Self-Esteem

No one can make you feel inferior without your consent.
—Eleanor Roosevelt

We need to return to the issue of power to understand our life experience as women and minority persons. Historically and currently, many women and minority persons have been stripped of their personal power by more powerful people and social systems. Regardless of the gains that have been made regarding equality for all, the view that women and minority persons have less value and importance has not died its final death.

Self-esteem is often hindered for women and minority persons by:
- ✓ The experience of having less power
- ✓ Being controlled by cultural socialization
    - Culture's view of value
    - Stereotypes
- ✓ Toxic relationships
- ✓ Occupational power differences

- ✓ Religious teachings
- ✓ Irrational guilt

❖ **The experience of having less personal power**

In different environments and in varying degrees of inequality, society is divided into dominant people who have more power and subordinate persons who have less power. The subordinate position of women and minority persons often involves being devalued, told how and what to think, feel, act, believe, and value in most areas of their lives: socially, intellectually, emotionally, sexually, economically, and spiritually. It is blatant and abusive control when women and minority persons are directly threatened or forced into submission and compliance to satisfy and benefit more powerful, controlling people or groups. Less obvious is the subtle but powerful socialization of women and minority persons that creates feelings of being inferior and having less value. When women and minority persons are controlled, either blatantly or in less obvious ways, they are powerless to make their own choices, form their own identities, take charge of their lives, and develop healthy self-esteem. When less powerful people are taught, treated, and conclude that they have less power, they become less able to confront the people and the systems that control them. As a result, power inequities continue generation after generation.

When women or minority persons are abused and oppressed, self-esteem is not even a consideration. What consumes personal energy is providing safety, food, and shelter for themselves and their children. Some controlling behaviors, such as physical and sexual abuse, threats, extreme verbal abuse, intimidation, and humiliation are so severe that women and minority persons need assistance from law enforcement to stay physically safe. Although the control may not involve violence or a potential for being harmed, there are other types of controlling behaviors directed toward women and minorities that lower self-esteem, including anger expressed aggressively, sarcasm, blame, exaggerating, distorting information, discounting or minimizing, directing, commanding and warning, frequent fault-finding, and name-calling. Controllers often have an attitude of entitlement, and feel that they deserve compliance to their demands. (Rogne, C., *Who's Controlling You? Who Are You Controlling? – Strategies for Change, 2010)*.

People who are controlled have predictable *emotions*, such as:

- Feeling powerless
- Feeling angry and resentful
- Feeling exhausted, discontented, and emotionally empty
- Feeling trapped in the controlling relationship
- Feeling that they can do nothing right for the controller
- Feeling inferior, inadequate, and unworthy
- Feeling a growing dislike and often hatred for the controller
- Feeling a desire to escape
- Feeling, "There is something wrong with me."

Women and minority persons are often viewed as less intelligent by controllers. Many women have experienced turmoil and high levels of stress in their primary relationships and in their work setting because of their intelligence, intuitiveness, and global vision. To be accepted, to please others, and to avoid conflict, some women *hide* their intelligence, put on a facade of helplessness, and do not express their emotions. Women and minorities often underestimate their abilities, whereas controllers often overestimate what they are capable of doing. When women and minority persons are no longer willing to be controlled and start to confront, conflict often occurs or ongoing conflicts escalate.

Rather than believing that they are *innately inadequate* as controllers would like them to believe, women and minority persons are *frequently placed at a disadvantage* because of power inequities. When women and minority persons become aware that many of the conflicts and obstacles they experience in their lives are not caused by an *inadequacy within themselves*, but rather how power is often unequal and used against them, they are empowered, even though they may not be able to change the power inequities. They can, however, stop believing they are at fault and stop internalizing the manipulative blame and criticisms directed at them by controllers. If they, themselves, have a degree of personal power and are not in danger of being harmed, they can confront or do less enabling of controlling behaviors in their personal relationships and in their work settings. They can also help other less powerful people to identify controllers' tactics and stop assigning the cause for their oppression to themselves.

- Joyce shares:

    I have often felt that women are like Avis rent-a-car advertising, and because they are second, could say the same thing, "We try harder!" It seems like a lot has changed, but nothing has changed as far as women's power, how we are treated, and the lower wages we receive. We talk a lot about equality in America, but there is often inequality, and we, as women, are certainly not number one. But the number ones, with all of their power, are doing the majority of harm to others that goes on in our society. We don't read much about women being the perpetrator of domestic violence or sexual abuse. That is usually done by men who are controlling and demanding. So much of our emotional pain is about having power used against us, and how powerful people have so many privileges in so many areas. But most of us try hard to make everything work in our relationships and with our children. It took me a long time to understand how we are placed at a disadvantage because of having unequal power. Just like I have thought so many times, we are much like the advertising by Avis. We are second in many ways, so we try harder.

Many women and minority persons are creative in circumventing and escaping the controlling tactics, at least to some degree. First, they realize that they are not always wrong or inferior and that their skills, interests, and priorities are important. In their growing awareness, they are learning to view themselves as being competent and valuable and know that they are equal to others, even though they may be treated as unequal. It is also empowering for women and minority persons to realize that being viewed as less powerful and subordinate or less valuable does not make it true, unless they agree to this false notion.

There are strong, creative, and resilient women and minority persons, especially those who are educated and have financial resources and marketable skills, who are successful, despite the fact that they are challenged with varying degrees of control, oppression, disadvantage, and obstruction. Educated women and minority persons often intentionally enter work systems that are equal opportunity—in pay, power, and prestige. In these work settings, they are respected and paid according to their skill level. Or, if they do work in systems where inequality exists, they discover ways to survive. There are also women and minority persons who create their own work systems and are successful entrepreneurs. Although it is not always possible, being independent allows for their freedom of expression, talents, and intelligence.

Being controlled by cultural socialization diminishes self-esteem

Cultural socialization involves learning the attitudes, values, and acceptable and preferable behaviors of our culture. Though cultural socialization promotes positive values, such as basic pro-social behaviors, it also promotes attitudes and behaviors that are oppressive to people. Enculturation is not like the education we experience in school through textbooks and formal instruction. It is far more subtle, conveyed through advertisements, television, movies, music, and other types of media. We typically do not realize we are being programmed with culturally influenced attitudes, ways of thinking, and ways of behaving. Because our cultural mental programming is usually not in our conscious awareness, we seldom discern what is true or false, healthy or unhealthy, and what is useful or problematic in what we unknowingly learn from our culture.

Culture's view of personal value

From a cultural view, our sense of having value is based on:

- Age, race, and gender
- Prestigious occupation or profession
- Social status
- Wealth, possessions, and luxuries
- Physical attractiveness
- Athletic ability
- Special talents
- Inherited social status from parents who are wealthy, famous, and/or talented
- Being extroverted
- Personal achievements
- Achievements of a spouse, children, or relatives

Whether or not we have any or all of these attributes, we are likely to experience a time when our value, as viewed by society, diminishes or disappears. We become less physically attractive as we grow older according to cultural standards, our personal achievements may no longer describe us, we may lose a job, retire, have financial difficulties, or be incapacitated in ways that make it difficult, if not impossible, to be mobile or self-sustaining. If we accept society's version of value and being worthy, our self-esteem and sense of value will decrease when we experience these types of losses.

Our culture silently assigns value based on **doing** rather than **being**:

Cultural view: Self-esteem and having value as a person is based on our **doing**. When value is assigned for *doing* rather than *being*, many people, such as the elderly, women, children, and minority persons, are viewed as having less value.

Spiritual view: Self-esteem and having value as a person is simply based on **being** a person. No one is inferior. All people have equal value.

Society's view of personal value and worth is markedly different than believing that all people have equal value, with no persons viewed as having *more* innate value. Obviously there are different levels of achievement among people. We may be in different places on our life journey. However, everyone has value and the value is equal to all others.

Cultural stereotypes lower self-esteem

Cultural stereotypes encourage women to be passive, selfless, meek, adaptable, compliant, nice, attractive, slim, and to put their efforts into pleasing others. If these cultural directives are followed, at the expense of self, they are contrary to mental health principles. Being passive and adaptable are characteristics that are beneficial to more powerful people, who will not be faced with resistance and confrontation when they are demanding compliance to their requests.

Women are expected to be caring and compassionate to others, but not for themselves. They are often personally attacked by derogatory names when they challenge controllers' viewpoints, power inequities, or policies that favor dominant, powerful people. The rates of depression are higher for women, and this may be a result of being *oppressed* in ways that limit their choices and limit their lives.

There is a strong cultural directive for women and minority persons to *not* express their anger, create conflict, complain, or criticize, which are expectations that support those in power. Less powerful people are often discredited when they express anger. Not expressing feelings, including anger, creates a vulnerability to headaches, ulcers, heart problems, asthma, insomnia, and cancer. Anger is a natural response to being mentally, verbally, emotionally, sexually, and physically abused, but so often, women or minority persons who are physically or sexually assaulted feel *guilty* rather than angry. Feeling guilty rather than angry is an indicator of the power of subtle and oppressive socialization. If cultural stereotypes are followed, women and minority persons become less capable of confronting the people who are controlling them and adversely affecting their lives.

❖ **Toxic relationships**

When we are in a primary relationship with a controller who wields power over us, teamwork and mutual problem-solving is nonexistent. When power is unequal in relationships, the ongoing feelings that are generated are *anger, dishonesty, fear, and distance.* Persons who are controlled become **angry** when their life is being orchestrated by controllers, and controllers are angry when people don't respond immediately to meet their demands. Less powerful people are often **dishonest** with controllers, and withhold information because people **fear** controllers' anger, which is too often expressed in ways that are frightening. There is emotional **distance** in controlling relationships, causing a lack of meaningful or endearing communication. Controlling relationships are toxic relationships, which destroy self-esteem.

Though there have been some changes, our culture subtly teaches women that the way to be normal and have worth is to marry a man and have children. However, even though a woman may marry, have children, and present herself to the outside world as happy, marriage is often disappointing. Women usually expect their primary relationship to be emotionally connected, cooperative, and mutually supportive. What they often experience is that husbands are often emotionally unavailable, are controlling, do not function as a team, and expect to be supported and receive attention, even though they often do not reciprocate. Whereas males are often focused on sexual intimacy, females are more interested in emotional intimacy, which is viewed as less important. Women are often criticized for expressing themselves emotionally and called *too emotional.*

Since women are stereotypically viewed in our culture as responsible for making relationships work, despite the fact that it takes both partners to have a good relationship, they often feel guilty and accept the blame if their relationship deteriorates or their husband has an affair. Women often stay in a marriage with a controlling partner because they know that if they left, the control would escalate, and/or they could not support themselves financially. Rather than leave, they often enable the controlling behaviors in efforts

Challenges to Women and Minority Persons' Self-Esteem

to prevent conflict and financial hardship that is apt to affect their children.

It is not unusual for women to be surprised when they are treated more respectfully in their work setting, by both males and females, compared to how they are treated in their marriages.

- Roberta shares:

    When my ex-husband asked me why I never re-married, I was honest with him and told him that I would never subject myself to an experience like that again. He was very controlling and there were times that I thought he may get out of control and be physically abusive. He would be so critical and convinced me that I was always the problem. Then I changed jobs and had a boss that was very respectful to me and valued my work. He would ask me for my opinion on certain situations. I was blown away, and thought it would be so nice to be treated as respectfully in my marriage. I started to see things more clearly about the control and realized that the control came from his insecurity and feeling inadequate. That helped me to ignore his criticisms and comments. But then the conflict escalated because he couldn't get me to feel bad and cry. I concluded that there would be no changes and I decided to leave him. I created a new life, and have never regretted my decision.

❖ **Occupational power differences**

There is still a wage discrepancy between men and women for comparable types of work positions. Women and minority persons often work in the areas of service, such as teaching, care taking, organizing, cleaning, and offering supportive services to managers and administrators. These occupations are important in a society, but are jobs that typically have lower compensation and prestige.

Women and minority persons who work in traditional male professions often experience discrimination, harassment, lower salaries, and are more closely scrutinized. When working under these conditions, it is predictable that persons are more likely to become emotionally compromised and highly stressed. If they start to reveal weakness in the work setting, they are readily discredited and determined to be incapable of handling the job.

- Amy shares:

    I am a physician and was shocked when I was harassed when I was in a group medical practice with men. They would say demeaning things, like "Here comes the queen of medicine," and disband when I was anywhere near their chat groups in the hallways. The same male physicians that called me crazy were the ones who would be remiss in patient care and more than once, I rescued their patients. I was very stressed and felt like I was living on the edge. Looking back at medical school, we should have had a course in power dynamics in the medical field, because it is experienced so often by other female physicians. It is incredibly confusing and creates a lot of despair, to the point of wanting to leave the profession. The power differences between males and females still exist, even though there are more women becoming physicians. But once I discovered the many ways that controlling power works, I stopped believing that I was crazy. That was my first step and it was a huge step! Eventually I was able to create my own work system in a specialty medical field, so I no longer had to deal with the harassment that I experienced working with male colleagues, which I had never expected and was ill-prepared to handle.

- Natalie shares:

    In my job as a team supervisor, I felt that I was well respected and paid what I deserved to be paid. I don't think I was paid any less than men, except for the CEOs that were earning tons of money. But I would get pretty upset when there was yet another directive about cutting staff and eliminating overtime, which I knew only meant a little savings compared to the wages that our bosses were getting, who were men. I am sure that they never took a cut in wages. That never made sense to me, but I knew that was how the system worked, even though it was unfair and that customer satisfaction was supposed to be our first concern, even though when we cut staff, we were doing the exact opposite of what we were saying was our priority.

Research confirms that men are much more likely to be offered leadership positions because selection processes are often covert and put males at an advantage over women. Men are also provided more mentoring as they transition into higher administrative roles. Women are limited in opportunities and are less likely to reach executive levels. Despite their skills, education, and talents, women are more likely to be managed by a supervisor, or work in secondary management roles.

When women and minority persons complain about inequities, they are often accused of feeling sorry for themselves. Rather than having their legitimate concerns and complaints acknowledged, they are often labeled and called aggressive when they are assertive, and stubborn and uncooperative when they disagree. Many women and minority persons cannot afford to put their job at risk so they remain quiet and compliant, which ensures that the existing inequitable power structures remain the same.

We need only look at the representation in the 112th United States

Congress to see the inequality in positions of power. Seventeen of the 100 U.S. Senators are women. In the House of Representatives, there are 73 women out of 435 representatives. Women comprise only 17% of both the Senate and the House of Representatives.

❖ Religious teachings

Jesus' teachings and actions clearly showed a respect and equality for all persons, including women. However, patriarchal attitudes have influenced organized religion for centuries. Women are often portrayed as evil, seductive, and inferior. The amount of guilt generated by the doctrine of original sin is incalculable and is not Scripture-based. These guilt-based tactics render people, especially women, feeling inferior, which is a root of low self-esteem. Questioning doctrines and practices in organized religion is seldom encouraged, which is a subtle way to control people. One of the reasons why people are choosing to leave organized religion and discover other spiritual paths is that Jesus' words and actions seem to have gotten lost in some forms of organized Christianity.

❖ Irrational guilt

Because of how women are socialized, they are not very good at feeling angry, but they are very good at feeling guilty. Women are expected to be understanding, compassionate, helpful, empathetic, and willing to alter schedules, preferences, priorities, and activities in order to meet others' needs or requests. They often try to be a twenty-four-hour, one-stop shopping center, having whatever is needed for anyone who makes a request in efforts to not upset anyone and make all situations go smoothly. Many women feel guilty for confronting, disagreeing, being angry, or refusing to be overextended. Because of being bogged down by irrational, needless, invalid guilt, they often continue to act out of feelings of obligation and what they believe is a duty.

Women are often the main caretaker in the family out of choice, necessity, or a response to the expectations of our culture. With this responsibility, along with the feeling of *not being good enough*, mothers feel guilty when bringing their children to daycare; they feel guilty when their children have behavior or learning problems, and feel responsible and guilty when their children experiment with alcohol and drugs. Women feel guilty when the house isn't orderly, the laundry piles are high, the garbage is overflowing, and there is no milk in the refrigerator. When fathers are distant or controlling, many mothers try very hard to make up for the nurturing their children do not receive from their fathers and feel guilty when they are not successful. And often, all of their guilt is hidden within them and is never discussed with others. The accumulated guilt may cause emotional, physical, and spiritual harm.

- Meghan shares:

    I felt guilty when I took my preschool children to daycare, as it was usually a tearful experience for them. But we needed my salary to work, although I didn't have much left of my paycheck after I paid for daycare. So I often wondered what I should do, but my husband was pretty insistent that I work. I know I would feel guilty if I didn't bring home a salary. I am a pretty intelligent person, but can't seem to let go of my crazy guilt!

It is not uncommon that when women demonstrate their personal power, the outcome is feeling guilty because of criticism from men and often from other women. In administrative positions, where there can be difficult decisions regarding people's lives, such as having to terminate someone from their employment, women in management and administration walk a fine line between acting decisively and still being responsive to the expectation that they be emotionally warm and nurturing. Very often, when women in management confront and terminate employees, they feel guilty and alienated from others.

When women and minority persons start refusing to accept guilt and stop doing things for people that they should be doing for themselves, they are often called selfish, self-pitying, uncooperative, and stubborn, as a manipulative way to have them return to their passive behaviors, be willing to neglect themselves, and invest their energies into nurturing others.

One of the aspects of a low self-esteem recovery process is refusing to feel guilty for no actual reason. To do this, we have to understand the difference between valid guilt based on rational thinking and toxic guilt, which is created by our irrational beliefs that trigger irrational guilt. This is thoroughly discussed in Chapter 6.

> **Women and minority persons may be *unable* to change power inequities, but it is empowering to become more aware and understand their experiences in the framework of power and control. If the power used to control does not pose physical threats, power inequities can be confronted. Or, it may be possible to circumvent the control by being credible, assertive and creative. However, it is only by working together, that women and minority persons we be able to right the wrongs that abusive power continually creates.**

Chapter 4

The Journey of Recovery and Personal Growth

Be not afraid of growing slowly; be afraid only of standing still.
Chinese Proverb

If we are considering making a commitment to a recovery and growth process, we probably would like to have a description of what is required, what is likely to be experienced, and how we are going to feel as we progress through the stages. A recovery process may start because we are experiencing an emotional crisis, which often forces us to focus on ourselves and draw from our deep, inner strength, which may be a new experience for us. Some of us began a recovery process because we were exhausted from being in emotional turmoil and realized that staying in our emotional pain was more frightening than making changes in our thoughts, attitudes, and behaviors.

The personal growth process involves looking *within* and taking time to reflect on our lives, goals, and what we want to experience in life. In our culture, we are not encouraged to take a journey within or talk about deep feelings, fears, values, or spirituality. Because of this, many of us do not know our inner thoughts and feelings. If we are committed to beginning any type of recovery process, including recovering from low self-esteem, we need to stop avoiding our feelings by using chemicals, being excessively busy with activities to distract us from ourselves, or seeking out other persons to take care of us and fill our emptiness.

Recovery and personal growth is a *process* that occurs over time, contrary to the *instant* mentality that we experience in our culture—instant coffee, cash, and burgers. We cannot instantly raise our awareness, change behaviors, and recover from low self-esteem. In a healing and personal growth process, we need to take all the time necessary so that our recovery and personal growth is authentic.

A recovery process starts by moving out of our denial, or our unawareness. We continually learn more about who we are, how we have been influenced by other people and society, and what has transpired within our lives. Self-reprimand and rigidity arrest our recovery and healing process. If we accept rather than resist the recovery and personal growth process, we naturally move toward greater wholeness of being.

Our recovery process is usually not a steady and forward process. We often take two steps forward and one step backward, and then resume our forward movement. As we grow, we understand our experiences in greater clarity. Most of us need to hear, read, or experience information more than once before we are able to effectively incorporate new learning into our thoughts and behaviors. In addition, we might need to hear, read, or experience information, insights, or truths in *different* ways. We gain understanding and insight into ourselves through a *variety* of sources and experiences. It is also true that we are more ready to learn at certain times in our lives than in other times. We have all had the experience of hearing or reading information that we did not initially understand or, perhaps, were simply not interested in at the time, but later, we clearly understood and valued the same information. We were more receptive to the lesson, information, or *truth* at a later time in our lives.

Having words for our experiences

There are times when we have emotions that we have difficulty expressing with language. Our feelings seem to be undifferentiated and roam around in our minds. When we discover a word to describe the feeling, we can then *pin it down* and make it real to us.

Here are examples of words that might be difficult to describe regarding our feelings or experiences:

- Inadequate: I feel inadequate and I think I am not as good as other people.
- Vulnerable: I feel emotionally fragile and am afraid of being hurt.
- Risk: I'm taking a risk and am not sure of the outcome.
- Self-doubt: I feel like I may not be capable of doing what I need to do.
- Control: I am being controlled and feel trapped.
- Over-extended: I am doing too many things for too many people.
- Challenged: This is difficult but I think I can do this.
- Feeling adrift: I'm not sure where I am going in my life.
- Feeling empty: I feel nothing, like a void.
- Guarded: I am not sure that I can trust you, so I am guarded.

Naming the feeling clarifies it. We have an "aha!" revelation. This may happen through a flash of insight, or we may hear a word and know that it is the exact word that explains our feeling or situation. When we *name* the feeling, we can then work with the feeling. It is ours. We can take charge. We have more choices as to what we are going to do, based on the feeling. We may say, "Oh, that's what's happening. I get it. Now I can deal with it."

Raising awareness about feelings

Some of us have purposely stayed away from our feelings to avoid emotional pain. Recovery and personal growth involves learning to treat all of our feelings as trusted friends, even the more difficult feelings like anger, jealousy, and resentment. In our growth process, we will, at first, feel *more* feelings, and then we will feel *better*.

Suggestions on how to acknowledge and work with feelings:

- Pay attention to your feelings
- Accept all of your feelings, including the difficult and negative emotions
- Listen to the message that your feelings bring
- Write about your feelings in a journal, for greater understanding and clarification
- Appreciate the growth you are experiencing in learning to acknowledge and express your feelings appropriately

A healthy recovery and growth process is moving from wherever we start to a healthier level of well-being. The learning involved in a personal growth journey is not just an intellectual experience. Personal growth learning is also an *emotional* experience. Knowing on a *head* level is not the same as knowing on a *heart* or emotional level. Emotional learning is deeper and more poignant, often changing our lives in remarkable ways. It is a connection with our *inner* truth. If we have emotional knowing, and say to ourselves, "I am lovable and capable," we truly *believe* that we are lovable and capable and treat ourselves with the utmost respect and kindness.

Journaling

Writing in a journal is a good way to discover more about ourselves, to clarify what we are feeling and thinking, identify personal issues, and design our goals. When we journal, we want to be totally relaxed and have plenty of time without interruption. In our private journal, we can write from our heart about our deepest thoughts and feelings.

You may want to make certain that your journal is kept in a private and secure place so that you know that no one else will be reading it. There is no right or wrong way to write in your journal. You don't have to censor your words, be reasonable, nice, have neat handwriting, or have correct grammar. You can be completely honest in your private journal. No one is going to read your journal and make judgments on you, so you don't have to be guarded. Your writing may turn into angry scribbling, pictures, or diagrams.

Be in a comfortable and quiet place when you journal. Before writing, breathe deeply several times to relax. By putting your emotions into words, you will be able to view your feelings as being momentarily external to yourself, which provides some objectivity. You may want to save your journal writings to read at a later time in your life.

Stages in a recovery and personal growth process

We have to work our own recovery process, rather than depending on others to heal our low self-esteem and emotional discontent. A recovery and personal growth process has common stages, but we travel through them in our own unique way.

Stage 1: Questioning and raising our awareness

Questioning and self-reflecting help us to understand ourselves more fully. In this personal growth stage, we question what we learned about ourselves from parents, extended family, friends, clergy, and other significant persons in our life. We may question aspects of our cultural socialization, our religion, the political and legal process, and how power is unequally distributed. Questioning leads to greater awareness. As a result, we may reject some of the trends of society, resist following the crowd, refuse to spend time doing meaningless activities, stop going along to get along, and start designing our life around our own values and priorities.

- Barb shares:

    When I started really questioning the things that I had learned, I was amazed. I was raised to be passive and to not rock the boat. Be nice all the time. Well, that didn't get me anywhere except feeling crummy about myself. And then I started questioning my religion and there was a lot of guilt. Every Sunday we would say that we had done sins of commission and sins of omission and so I always felt that I didn't do anything good for God. And that probably meant I was a bad person and wasn't going to heaven. And then I started questioning why wealthy people seem to have an advantage in the legal system and in politics. That led to me questioning about how there is a lot of talk about equal rights for everyone in America, but that isn't always true. I'm still questioning and will continue!

Stage 2: Sorting out and discarding what is false and life-diminishing

Low self-esteem recovery involves recalling our past experiences to discover what we learned and what conclusions we made about ourselves. For some of us, we will feel anger because we were emotionally, verbally, and/or physically abused. Even though we may not have suffered abuse in our childhoods, we may recall unhealthy directives or reprimands by our parents, teachers, and clergy. We formed certain beliefs about ourselves, based on these interactions with adults.

After we become aware of how we were mentally programmed, the next step is to rigorously discard information, attitudes, and beliefs that are false and life-diminishing and that sabotage our self-esteem. Among the false learning that needs to be discarded are the negative beliefs about ourselves, such as believing that we are inadequate, incompetent, and "There is something wrong with me."

Stage 3: Feeling an emotional emptiness

This stage in our personal growth process involves feelings of emptiness because we have discarded negative, misleading, life-diminishing, and false beliefs about ourselves. We have probably come to mistrust some of our society's organizations and institutions. We may have detached from toxic relationships. We may feel empty because we are in a recovery process and miss our substance, activity, or person that was involved in our addictive process. Familiar ways of thinking and behaving have changed. As a result there is less drama in our lives, which in the past consumed an excessive amount of time and energy. Feeling emotional emptiness is *positive* because it indicates that emotional work has actually happened, and that there has been a mental, emotional, and spiritual clearing of false notions and illusions. This empty place within ourselves can now be filled with true beliefs and more positive ways of thinking and behaving.

Stage 4: Learning to think in ways that are life-fostering

New ways of thinking happen naturally as a result of acquiring new knowledge and skills and changing negative thinking to positive thinking. Our thinking becomes more visionary, less rigid, and more altruistic. By revising our thinking, we will come to the realization that we are valuable, we are an important part of the world, we have a responsibility to ourselves as well as others, we have meaning and purpose, and our essence is good, precious, and valuable. All of these positive changes in the way we think will result in healing and growing spiritually.

- Melvin writes:

    I was able to do this quite easily, but I didn't realize how my friendships would be affected and how I became almost counter-cultural. I was no longer willing to waste my time and money doing meaningless activities like my friends. I became more interested in protecting the environment. I became more generous with my money, but I always gave it directly to people rather than the large agencies that claimed to be charity, but offered huge salaries to their directors. Gradually, I met new friends who were on my same wavelength, questioning many things and interested more in ideas rather than gossiping about what other people were doing. I came away from these conversations filled with energy, enthusiasm, and new ideas. I liked the feelings a lot, so I kept on going to where I seemed to be guided, and life became more meaningful and peaceful.

Stage 5: Integrating

Beliefs, spiritual principles, thoughts, values, feelings, and behaviors are integrated in this stage, which is movement toward health and wholeness. Personal authenticity, integrity, and wisdom are valued. Actions are based on internal directives rather than a response to external expectations. Transcending the idea of what is male or what is female, we view ourselves as members of the human family who have integrated the best characteristics of each gender.

In this stage, we are inner-directed and our thought processes are in higher levels of awareness. We understand that humans are truly mind, body, spirit, and emotional beings. We believe that we are all interconnected and that if one person is being oppressed, we are all affected. Conversely, if one person is healing, growing, and becoming enlightened, all people are positively affected.

Stage 6: Transforming

Personal transformation involves thinking on a higher level of consciousness and re-designing parts of our lives accordingly. The healing and recovery journey has involved *un-learning* the negative attitudes, illusions, and beliefs that are false and life-diminishing, and changing our thinking and self-talk to be more positive. Transformation also involves looking to *ourselves* as the major source of happiness and growth and discovering what is fulfilling and meaningful. In a transformation process we realize that we have no obligation to spend time with toxic people or to respond to their every request. We may change our relationships and leave energy-takers, despite the pressure to stay. We now gravitate toward people whose energies are more positive and life-promoting.

In this stage, we no longer feel inferior, and we relate to ourselves and others in more caring, honest, positive, and healthy ways. Our transformation has ushered in the realization that our happiness does not depend upon how people respond to us or meet our needs, but upon the nature of our inner world. We learned through both pain and joy that the ultimate responsibility for recovering from low self-esteem is ours, though when we were struggling, we may have wished that others could have done it for us. We increasingly realized that we are marvelous and unique persons, and that our *true center* is good. We have a commitment to our continued recovery and growth.

Our transformation process results in *new personal freedoms*—freedom from negative thinking, self-reprimands, resentments, self-created fears—free of all of the false information that we learned about ourselves, and free from our self-sabotaging thoughts and behaviors. Our transformation involves emotional healing and evolving toward spiritual values, including love, courage, compassion, acceptance, honesty, and truth. Our thoughts change from, "There is something wrong with me," to a sincere belief that *"I am lovable, capable, and one of God's miracles."* We experience freedom to *be* all that we are meant to be.

Healthy personal growth involves *both* processes of looking inward and reaching outward. We do not become stuck in ourselves if we respect, honor, and go with our natural recovery and personal growth process. We reach out to others in healthy ways and actively share our skills and strengths out of choice and a feeling of abundance and gratitude.

> **Recovery and personal growth involves healing and growing from within. There are stages in a healing and growth journey that involve achieving greater awareness, rejecting false learning, and learning to love and respect ourselves as well as all others.**

Chapter 5

Healing from Harmful Experiences in Childhood

> *The truth is that our finest moments are most likely to occur when we are feeling deeply uncomfortable, unhappy, or unfulfilled. For it is only in such moments, propelled by our discomfort, that we are likely to step out of our ruts and start searching for different ways or truer answers.* —Author unknown

We may have experienced trauma in our childhood that was emotionally crushing, such as physical, sexual, emotional, or verbal abuse. The more severe our harmful experiences, the more difficult it is to recover emotionally and rebuild our self-esteem. Though it may not be possible for everyone, working with a competent therapist is the most effective way to recover from harmful experiences and traumatic losses that happened in our childhood.

When recalling memories about our childhood, we are not blaming parents or other adults. But we have a right to explore our childhood experiences and take an objective look at what happened to us that caused our current emotional pain and low self-esteem. As hurtful memories and the people who were involved come to mind, we are likely to become angry and sad. However, by recalling our experiences, we can start a healing process, rather than letting our emotional wounds continue to fester and adversely affect our mental, emotional, spiritual, and physical health.

We may not have experienced abuse or trauma in our childhood, but we may have felt abandoned because a parent left us or because of a separation, divorce, or death. Or, we may have felt abandoned when a parent or both parents were emotionally unavailable because they were using alcohol or drugs, participating in addictive activities, or spending excessive time watching television and playing video games. Children often think that they must have done something wrong if they do not feel loved, or feel abandoned. However, if we felt a lack of nurturing and caring, it was not our fault, and these experiences affected us at a deep emotional level. As children, we did not have the power to change the dysfunction in our families, nor could we leave our family and go search for more functional people to parent us.

In our childhood, we may have been frequently verbally abused with negative comments from adults. We may have been told that we didn't measure up to our parents' expectations, or we always created problems for our parents, or we were the cause of their marital problems. Talking about feelings, especially anger may have been discouraged or forbidden. We may have been told that good kids don't lie, even if we knew the punishment was going to be harsh and abusive when we told the truth. Perhaps we were told so many times that we were bad, we started to believe it. We may have decided that we were to blame when we were abused, and that there was something wrong with us when we couldn't protect a parent or sibling from being physically or emotionally harmed.

As children, we trusted adults, and were not able to sort out what was true or false or what was life-fostering or life-diminishing. We simply absorbed the negative statements that were directed toward us. **Rather than thinking that our low self-esteem is because we**

are innately inadequate and inferior, and it is our fault, it is important to realize that before we even knew what was happening, our esteem was either enhanced or diminished by the people who were supposed to love and nurture us. Knowing this fact, on both an intellectual and emotional level, is empowering because we can stop blaming ourselves if we struggle with low self-esteem.

When we are adults who have been wounded from harmful experiences in childhood, we may try to suppress our emotions and show a happy and functioning person to the outside world. However, we are likely to feel that something is gnawing at us, causing us to feel sad, anxious, and unsettled. We may have frightening nightmares, flashbacks, or recurring memories. Or, we may have an experience with someone who is overly critical, and we feel just like the frightened child we were many years ago, listening to a critical parent. Though we may think that the past is gone, our emotional wounds are like black and blue marks. If we bump the bruise, we become aware that it is still there and it still hurts.

The negative statements that were spoken to us in our childhood, from people we trusted, influence how we view ourselves in our adulthood. Even though we may have left our unjust criticizers, we continue to be overly critical of ourselves and believe that we are neither lovable nor capable. Because of being emotionally abused, we are at a high risk for *becoming* the negative labels that we may have heard repeatedly: a failure, a good-for-nothing, or a druggie. And despite our resolutions to have healthier behaviors than our dysfunctional parents, we often repeat the harmful behaviors, especially with our spouse and children.

As emotionally wounded adults, we may be uncertain as to what is *normal*. We may conclude that normal means the opposite of what we experienced in our childhood. Our healing brings the realization that normal means that people who claim to love us don't cause hurtful or haunting experiences and memories. In a safe home environment, children play and laugh, and when they are tired, they can go to bed without fear, shame, guilt, or confusion.

The emotionally healing grieving process

Many adults go through a grieving process to heal from the emotional wounds that occurred in their childhood. Whether our grief involves painful experiences in our childhood or losses of significant persons, our emotional healing involves working through the stages of grief, which are denial, anger, bargaining, depression, and acceptance. All of the emotional stages and feelings are a natural process within us for healing, but if we ignore or suppress our feelings, or are abusing alcohol or drugs, the healing process of grieving is hindered or arrested completely. When we do not go through a healthy grieving process, we are vulnerable to emotional and physical illness.

When we are devastated by a loss of a significant person through death or divorce, or experience an emotional crisis, it is important to increase our level of self-nurturance:

- Avoid addictive substances or activities
- Give yourself time to emotionally heal
- Seek out and share with others who are experiencing grief
- Accept caring and support from others
- Be kind and gentle to yourself
- Give your body extra rest
- Let yourself feel your painful emotions
- Keep physically active as much as possible
- Pray
- Read what is inspiring and provides comfort and hope
- Schedule special activities for Sundays, holidays, and long weekends

Healing from Harmful Experiences in Childhood

- Write in a journal to clarify your thoughts and feelings
- Keep routine patterns in your daily living as much as possible
- Be open to seeking professional help
- Keep major decisions to a minimum or postpone them temporarily
- Do something that you enjoy, like having lunch with a special friend or going for a Sunday drive to admire the beauty of nature.
- Surround yourself with things that are alive: new plants, pets, or fresh flowers
- If there are people you need to forgive, be willing to forgive them
- When you are ready, add new interests and friends to your life

The following is a description of the grieving stages, which involve different amounts of time for each individual. We may want to reach out for support during our grieving by participating in a support group or working with a therapist or clergy, especially if our loss was traumatic and severely affected our lives.

Stage 1: Denial. Denial is meant to give us time to deal with a shock or loss. It is an emotional stage that is meant to be temporary, but some people stay in denial for a long period of time. Staying in denial is a way of avoiding feelings. When we stay in denial, there are certain behaviors that are common, including:

- ✓ Focusing on others to avoid feelings
- ✓ Over-working, over-eating, over-spending
- ✓ Withdrawing from other people
- ✓ Exhaustive physical exercise
- ✓ Fun and pleasure-seeking to avoid feelings

63

Self-Esteem

- ✓ Putting on a facade that everything is fine
- ✓ Playing false roles, such as being strong, happy, or courageous
- ✓ Abusing alcohol or drugs
- ✓ Blocking memories
- ✓ Blaming others

When we move out of denial, we will naturally move into the next stage, which is anger.

Stage 2: Anger. The second stage of grieving involves anger. When we become aware that anger is part of a healing process, we may be surprised because it seems strange that anger can help us to emotionally recover from losses. We may be hesitant to work through the anger if we have learned and believe that anger is evil, against religious principles, or if we equate anger with aggressive anger. Some people have a difficult time acknowledging their anger. They describe their feelings as being hurt rather than being angry. Feeling hurt is more acceptable to them than feeling angry.

Reasons for grief-anger include being angry because we were abused as children, because a person left us, being angry at doctors, spouses, siblings, parents, the reality of mortality, angry because there are no answers to our questions, or angry at God. We may have our own unique reasons for being angry. Some of our anger may be irrational or misdirected, but *our anger is our anger* in this stage of grieving. We do not need to justify our anger, but we do need to deal with our angry emotions in healthy ways.

When we are working with our anger, we cannot hurt ourselves or others. If we internalize our anger, we hurt ourselves. If we lash out with our anger, we are disrespectful of others, and the angry interaction is likely to escalate. Verbally attacking others increases rather than diminishes our anger.

Working through anger can feel very frightening. However, we can go slow and trust our healing process. If we are grieving painful experiences in our childhood, we do not want to minimize the harm we experienced, but rather feel the full intensity of the anger. We may reach an emotional place where we feel like we are in the bottom of a pit of anger and despair and cry out in agonizing, emotional pain. With time, the angry feelings usually subside, giving us some emotional relief.

When we realize the importance of anger in the grieving process, we are more willing to acknowledge and work with this emotion. As our culture has evolved, we have lost some of our natural physical anger outlets, like beating rugs, digging potatoes, pitching hay, or walking miles to the nearest town to buy needed supplies. As a result, we have to create our own ways to effectively release our anger. Jogging and walking while pondering our anger may be helpful. Verbalizing our anger in private, combined with body movement, is effective when working with anger. Journaling is a good way to release anger. We can also transform the anger energy into creative projects or use the energy for helping others. Meditation is helpful, as is visualizing our anger leaving our minds and bodies.

If we avoid the anger stage, we may find ourselves:

- ✓ Abusing chemicals
- ✓ Losing control of our anger over trivial things
- ✓ Projecting the anger on innocent persons
- ✓ Being sarcastic and negative
- ✓ Having physical symptoms such as tense muscles, ulcers, chest pains, headaches, respiratory difficulties, or grinding teeth
- ✓ Having emotional struggles, such as depression and anxiety
- ✓ Compulsively involved in activities
- ✓ Over-working

Stage 3: Bargaining. Bargaining is wondering what we *could* have done, or what we *should* have done in the particular situation. In this stage, some people take on too much responsibility and generate a lot of guilt because they expect themselves to be able to do things that are beyond their control, such as being able to protect a parent from being abused or to change other types of family dysfunction. When we go through the bargaining stage, we need to be certain that we are not holding ourselves responsible for situations that we did not have the power to change, or excusing ourselves when we are not changing dysfunctional behaviors that are harming ourselves or others.

When we are healing from childhood wounds, this stage can be used as a perspective-taking stage. We can try to understand the experiences of whoever was abusive or neglectful. However, we do not need to make excuses for the abuse by thinking, "My father was abusive, *but* his father was the same way, so I shouldn't be angry." Perspective-taking is not protecting, minimizing, or excusing the abusive behavior we experienced. As a child, regardless of our behaviors, we did not deserve any type of abuse.

If we are grieving painful experiences in our childhood, these questions may be helpful:

- Did the person who was abusive grow up in an abusing family?
- Was he/she struggling with an addiction?
- Did she/he have intense levels of anger because of harmful experiences in their childhood?

Thinking about the background of the person who harmed us may help us to understand more about the people who were abusive to us. At some point in time, we may have the willingness to forgive those who harmed us.

Stage 4: Depression. The fourth stage in the grieving process is depression. This involves feeling sad, disconnected with parts of self, unmotivated, and lifeless. The experience of depression is evident in such symptoms as:

- ✓ Extended periods of crying
- ✓ Withdrawing from others
- ✓ Loss of interest in work or hobbies
- ✓ Over-sleeping or insomnia
- ✓ Loss or gain of appetite
- ✓ Drawn facial lines
- ✓ Feeling of being surrounded by a dark cloud
- ✓ Lack of motivation
- ✓ Difficulty in doing daily routines and tasks
- ✓ Feeling that *everything* is very difficult to do
- ✓ Feeling hopeless, helpless, and despairing

Journaling can be very helpful during the stage of depression, and it is a good way to stay active in our grieving process rather than trying to avoid feelings.

Stage 5: Acceptance. Acknowledging and accepting our loss is the last stage of grieving. We accept our loss, or we accept the fact that we endured harmful experiences. Though we would like to change what happened, we accept the fact that we cannot change the past. We are also accepting of the reality that some of our questions will not have answers. When we experience emotional acceptance, we will feel that we can slowly resume activities that are meaningful to us. Some courageous and caring people who have experienced tragedy reach out to others, organize groups, and help themselves to heal by helping others.

In this stage, we may feel:

- ✓ A feeling of peace
- ✓ Appreciation of what we *do* have
- ✓ Enjoyment of each new day
- ✓ A positive attitude about life
- ✓ Increased sensitivity toward others
- ✓ Motivated to reach out to others in emotional pain

The grieving process can be emotionally intense. It is best to take as much time as we need in each stage. However, we can't let ourselves become stalled in a grief stage for a long period of time. We need to keep moving emotionally at our own pace. How long it takes a person to even consider acceptance of what has happened depends on the person and the severity of the abuse or loss. There are abusive experiences and losses that are so severe and traumatic, it can take years to work through the pain, and some of the pain may always be with us.

Forgiveness

When we are grieving past abuse, neglect, abandonment, or other harmful experiences, forgiveness of our parents or other people who harmed us is necessary for emotional healing. If we are unwilling to forgive, we continue to live with anger, resentments, and bitterness. This means that the person we feel has harmed us still has power over us. We are more able to forgive when we have worked through the difficult emotions that are involved in the grieving process. Our forgiveness of those who negatively impacted our life is emotionally, physically, and spiritually healing. We know that we have truly forgiven when we have no negative emotional reaction upon encountering or having thoughts about the person who harmed us. It is like meeting a stranger who we are able to greet pleasantly. We have reached the point of blessed indifference.

> Who do I need to forgive?

Re-Parenting Ourselves

Re-parenting involves being a nurturing parent to ourselves by providing the healthy parenting we did not receive as children. When some of us think of the child we once were, we think of a joyful young person, running and skipping and enjoying life. For others, thinking about their young child brings up feelings of fear, sadness, loneliness, and abandonment. When we have emotional wounds from childhood, our inner child needs to be re-parented.

As an adult, we can provide assurance to our inner child that he/she will never have to be frightened again, which will provide a sense of security and safety. We can also communicate to our inner child that our love is unconditional and that as an adult, we are able to nurture in healthy ways, just like we nurture our own children, primary relationships, and close friends.

> **We need to always remember that having low self-esteem is not our fault. No person is innately inadequate and incompetent. Before we even knew what was happening, our esteem was either enhanced or diminished by the people who were supposed to love and nurture us.**

Chapter 6

Removing Self-Created Hindrances to Self-Esteem

*Healing takes courage, and we all have courage,
even if we have to dig a little to find it.*
—Tori Amos, singer, songwriter

Though our self-esteem may have been lowered because of the actions of *other* people, we are likely to have ways of thinking and behaving that sabotage *ourselves*. If we are in an active addiction process, self-esteem is adversely affected. We may still believe what dysfunctional parents or people told us in our childhoods and view ourselves in negative ways. The way we think may be faulty or irrational, although we may become defensive if we are confronted about our negative viewpoints and statements.

When we grow in self-awareness, we have the power to enhance our own self-esteem by opening our minds to new learning, thinking clearly, being honest with ourselves and others, and changing behaviors that are harmful to ourselves and others. We may think that we don't have enough time to work with ourselves because we are busy doing tasks. Some of us think that nothing can be changed, and a few of us hesitate to look inward in fear of what we may discover. At times, we may want to crawl back into our comfortable hide-outs and habits that keep ourselves away from our thoughts and feelings. But our inner truth will haunt us until we move forward. Our internal motivation is to move toward health and wholeness, but we need to intentionally provide the *willingness* to remove our self-sabotaging ways of thinking and behaving.

Recovery requires discarding what is life-diminishing:

- Addictions and addictive activities
- Past negative learning about ourselves
- Faulty thinking and negative self-talk
- Irrational beliefs and toxic guilt

❖ Recovering from addictions and addictive activities

Addiction can be generally defined as using a substance or participating in an activity that is creating a problem in one or more areas of our life. The substance or activity has control over us, rather than our being in control over the substance or activity. Our addiction often becomes our *first love,* and everything else in life is secondary. Our behaviors are often secretive, and we protect our addiction by being dishonest and defensive. Besides addictions to alcohol and mood-altering drugs, we can be addicted to work, money, sexuality, television, video games, and chat rooms. We can also be addicted to a relationship and wrap ourselves around a person in efforts to fix, control, be taken care of, or have a reason for existing. Addictive activities seem to *temporarily* remove our insecurities, numb our feelings, make problems seem to disappear, help us to relax, and fill our emptiness. But eventually, these activities involve paying a high emotional, physical, mental and financial price. Our relationships become increasingly dysfunctional, with high levels of stress and conflict.

◀ Self-Esteem

When we are controlled by an addiction, we are restless, irritable, and discontent. Our emotional growth and maturity are arrested. We eventually experience internal conflict because we know we are on a dead-end path, and our behaviors do not align with our values. To numb our gnawing, unpleasant, and persistent feelings, we continue with the addiction, or make resolutions such as "I'll quit tomorrow." When we fail at quitting, we feel like we have no options or bargain with ourselves that quitting is not important. We are so involved and obsessed with our addiction that we cannot imagine life without our substance, activity, or person. Despite knowing our behaviors are self-destructive, life-diminishing, and often life-threatening, we continue the behaviors. In Twelve-Step Program language, this is described as *the insanity of addiction*.

If we are actively involved in an addiction, starting a recovery process is necessary before we can make any significant and lasting changes within ourselves and in our relationships. Recovery involves restoring our health, relationships, integrity, sanity, and self-esteem. The program that is widely used for addictions and addictive activities is the Twelve-Step Program. The Twelve Steps are the same as mental health principles of well-being: being honest with self and others, taking personal responsibility for behaviors, being open and willing to make positive changes, making amends for harm done to others, and reaching out in service to others.

People are drawn to the Twelve-Step Program when they are in crisis and are *sick and tired of being sick and tired*. The Twelve-Step Program is similar to a therapeutic process with a counselor or support group, but without the cost, and a sponsor is available between meetings. The Program provides *tools for effective living* as we recover from an addiction that is cunning, baffling, powerful, and has the potential to destroy everything that is meaningful to us, including our lives. Higher Power is viewed as universal, benevolent, and a power greater than ourselves that can be experienced in our daily lives. In the Twelve-Step Program, the thoughts, behaviors, and experiences that go along with addiction are brought into the light as they are shared with trustworthy members who have had many of the same experiences.

Honesty is a cornerstone of the Twelve-Step Program. The recovery process is in the spirit of progress, not perfection. The acronym HOW is used, which stands for honesty, openness, and willingness. These are necessary attitudes and behaviors for a healthy and a sustaining sobriety. A continued and solid recovery program involves not only being *clean and sober*, but working the steps of the program, meeting with a sponsor, reading recovery literature, self-reflecting, and praying in ways that are meaningful to the individual person.

The Twelve Steps

1. We admitted we were powerless over alcohol (or other addiction)—that our lives had become unmanageable.
2. Came to believe that a Power greater than ourselves could restore us to sanity.
3. Made a decision to turn our will and our lives over to the care of God *as we understood Him.*
4. Made a searching and fearless moral inventory of ourselves.
5. Admitted to God, to ourselves, and to another human being the exact nature of our wrongs.
6. Were entirely ready to have God remove all these defects of character.
7. Humbly asked Him to remove our shortcomings.
8. Made a list of all persons we had harmed, and became willing to make amends to them all.
9. Made direct amends to such people wherever possible, except when to do so would injure them or others.

◁ Self-Esteem

10. Continued to take personal inventory and when we were wrong promptly admitted it.
11. Sought through prayer and meditation to improve our conscious contact with God *as we understood Him*, praying only for knowledge of His will for us and the power to carry that out.
12. Having had a spiritual awakening as the result of these steps, we tried to carry this message to alcoholics, and to practice these principles in all our affairs. (A.A. World Services, Inc).

People attending Twelve-Step meetings are not hesitant to share their thoughts, feelings, spirituality, and how Higher Power is working in their lives. It is healing and renewing to experience the energies of a Twelve-Step group, hear the honesty of the participants, and be totally accepted. Even if we are exhausted and unfocused, the spiritual energies in Twelve-Step meetings are uplifting. We feel energized and grateful for coming to a meeting and being in recovery, even though we may not have actively participated.

The Twelve Steps are based on the basic principles of all major religions. These include:

- God is love
- We are to treat others in ways that we would like to be treated
- All humanity is interconnected
- It is better to give than to receive
- We are to love our neighbor and ourselves

Spiritual awakening involves a heightened awareness of a connection to Higher Power, which the human spirit desires. Attraction, rather than promotion, is a guiding principle of the Twelve-Step Program. "Trust God, clean house, and help others" is the essence of the Twelve-Step Program.

There are about twenty-six different types of Twelve-Step groups, patterned after the Alcoholics Anonymous Twelve-Step Program. These groups include addictions such as gambling, narcotics, sex, and co-dependency. Since the behaviors are similar in each type of addiction, recovery involves actively working the Twelve Steps and, optimally, participating in a recovery group, reading the spiritual literature, and working with a sponsor. There are approximately fifteen million members in 150 countries holding Twelve-Step meetings in church basements, hospital conference rooms, school gyms, and other similar types of facilities.

- Ted shares:

    I abused alcohol for about ten years to forget my emotional pain and fill my emptiness. I never had a hangover, but my drinking was a ritual when coming home. I would drink enough to what I called *taking the edge off*, and then stop. Eventually, I realized I had a monkey on my back, because when I decided I needed to quit, I had many excuses and bargained with myself to justify drinking every night. I really felt I was a hopeless case and that I would always struggle with alcohol. Then I went to an AA meeting, and to my surprise, there were many people that looked just like me and had many of the same experiences. They were very friendly and welcoming. I felt very much at home. I will never forget how the speaker ended his talk that evening. He said, "Keep on coming to meetings. We will love you until you can learn to love yourself. Take one day at a time. Love God and go and serve."

By entering a recovery process for our addictions, we take a major step in preserving our health, our relationships, and enhancing our self-esteem.

◄ Self-Esteem

❖ Revising negative learning about ourselves

From statements made to us from parents and other adults, we may have concluded that we were inadequate, lazy, self-centered, too fat, too thin, not intelligent, too dramatic, not worthy of love, or other negative aspects about ourselves. If we are to recover from low self-esteem, we need to recall what was said to us and what we came to believe about ourselves. Some of the comments made to us were totally false, some may have been partially true, and some may be true, but we, ourselves, have to make that determination. Recalling, sorting out, revising, and discarding false or distorted information about ourselves is important because what we learned about ourselves is still affecting our lives today.

- Brad writes:

    I can't ever remember being told that I was loved by my parents or anyone else when I was young. I have been called lazy, no-good, stupid, and fat. I never knew what to expect when I got home, but most of the time there was a lot of arguing that led to screaming between mom and dad, or between dad and us kids. I never could please my dad. I got into a lot of trouble at school. I was a bully and it made me feel good when I could hurt someone else. It was hard for me to do school work because I was thinking about how terrible it was living in my family. I hated being at home. After school, I would go home and make myself sandwiches out of a whole loaf of bread. I took them to an abandoned shed and ate my sandwiches—peanut butter and sometimes bologna sandwiches, whatever was in the refrigerator. I felt worthless, and food helped the feelings go away. I still eat when I am stressed out, so being overweight has been a struggle for me most of my life. I keep feeling like all of the problems in my family were my fault. I have always felt like I was a screw-up. Well, it's true. I have lost several jobs and sometimes I just don't care about anyone or anything. Some days I don't want to get out of bed.

Like Brad, if we learned anything in our childhood that was contrary to the fact that we are lovable, capable, and valuable, we have to challenge and discard this false, life-diminishing information.

When we learn a particular fact and later discover that it is wrong, we can replace it with true information. Because our emotions are not involved, deleting the error and relearning is routine and effortless. But when the learning is *connected to our emotions* and is about *who we are as a person*, it is much more difficult to unlearn and change what we previously learned that was untrue. The process will feel like we are trying to do something that is next to impossible.

What makes emotional unlearning so difficult is that our thoughts of inadequacy or unworthiness create *actual* grooves in our brains. Thoughts and behaviors are memorized in our nerve cells. When we *unlearn* negative and false information that has emotional content, we are actually changing the grooves in our brain, which helps to explain why the process of deleting false learning and relearning truths about ourselves is so difficult. However, this process is possible because our brain is living and dynamic. We can discard false notions and replace them with information that is more accurate and positive. Our brain grooves will be upgraded, and our self-esteem will be a reflection of the positive changes in the beliefs we have about ourselves.

If we continue to go through life with negative and false views about ourselves, people may tell us about our positive qualities, but we often do not hear or we block out the positive statements because they are contrary to our beliefs. Rather than revise our thinking, we usually hold on to our negative beliefs about ourselves. However, to grow in self-esteem and self-acceptance, we need to delete the untruths in our minds, listen to positive feedback from others, and create new thoughts that are more accurate and life-fostering.

Whether it involves our mental, emotional, physical, or spiritual selves, we have to discover what is true for us and ***remove whatever is life-diminishing, false, and negative*** that we learned as we grew up, which adversely influences our lives on a daily basis. When we work an emotional process of clearing out or revising what is detrimental, we can then build a firm foundation for self-esteem, built on truth. Our emotional foundation will be strong so that we will be able to endure the challenges that life may present to us.

❖ **Changing faulty thinking and negative self-talk**

The way we think creates our reality. Faulty ways of thinking adversely affect our perceptions and beliefs. The errors we make in our thinking need to be identified and discarded because they are damaging to our self-esteem and emotional life. Faulty thinking is usually not in our awareness, but with some reflection, we can identify how we sabotage ourselves by our thoughts. Below are some of the common ways we fall in the trap of faulty thinking.

1. **Magnifying mistakes and minimizing affirmations.** After being criticized, we may ruminate about the criticism for several days. In contrast, when we receive a compliment, we often do not even hear or acknowledge it. We certainly don't wallow in affirmations like we wallow in the criticisms we receive. Rather than obsessing about mistakes, we need to take responsibility, make corrections, learn from them, let them go, and move on. With compliments and affirmations, we need to hear and savor them, not only with our ears but

with our hearts.

2. **Externalizing success and internalizing failure.** Many people attribute their success to luck rather than acknowledging the achievement as an outcome of their own efforts. When they experience failure, they often identify the cause of failure as being something wrong with *them*, rather than dysfunctional dynamics in a relationship or other factors that are beyond their control. These are irrational ways of thinking. We can learn to quietly acknowledge our successes and affirm ourselves for our efforts and achievements.

3. **Focusing on our 10% rather than our 90%.** We all have stronger and weaker areas, but we often focus on what is **wrong** with us rather than what is **right** with us. Examples of self-talk directed by our harsh inner critic are: "I'm worthless because I am a poor reader," or, "I'm inadequate because I'm not athletic, uninteresting, or too passive." This type of self-talk is treating ourselves unfairly. If we think rationally, there might be only ten percent of our behaviors that need changing. Most of us are responsible, respectful, and extend ourselves to others in healthy ways. If we place our focus on our weaknesses, they will grow stronger. If we place our focus on our strengths, they will help us to overcome our weaknesses. It is our choice.

4. **Expecting ourselves to be perfect.** Thinking that we need to be perfect will undoubtedly diminish our self-esteem because it is an impossible expectation. We are often directed by the "shoulds" that we generate in our minds, such as "I should be able to *learn* more quickly," or, "I should be better at soccer," or, "I should be more attractive or handsome."

We treat ourselves harshly when we make common mistakes and expect ourselves to be super-persons, able to do all things for everyone and do them perfectly. We can strive to be our best, but it is self-defeating to reprimand ourselves when our best is not perfect. When we relentlessly demand perfection of ourselves, we treat ourselves unfairly.

5. **Comparing ourselves to others in an unfair way.** When we compare ourselves to others, we are usually focused on people who we perceive as being in some way *ahead of us or better than us*. We fail to look at everyone, which means that we will never measure up, since our measuring procedure is unfair. We may think that others are more successful, more competent and skilled, more attractive, luckier, and have more value. The error in thinking is that we magnify the strengths of others and minimize our own. A better approach is to compare ourselves to *ourselves* and acknowledge our accomplishments and the progress we have made regarding our mental, emotional, physical, or spiritual health.

6. **Generalizing one failure to all parts of our life.** When we make a mistake or fail in one area of our life, we may generalize and feel like we are failures in *all* areas of our life. If we make a mistake at work, we might have thoughts such as, "I am so stupid!" and then generalize and have increasingly irrational and self-berating thoughts such as, "I'm not a good parent," or, "My in-laws hate me," or "I'm not a good person." Thoughts such as these take us down a road of self-condemnation based on a simple, correctable mistake. This is another way of self-sabotaging. Our challenge is to treat ourselves fairly, rationally, honestly, and respectfully, under all circumstances in life.

7. ***All or nothing*** **and** ***either/or*** **thinking is irrational.** When we use all or nothing thinking, and we are not totally successful at something, we think we are total failures. If we use either/or thinking, we are all good or we are all bad. If our relationships are not all good, they are bad. This is thinking in extremes. When we think that situations are *all or nothing*, or *either/or*, we rule out the *in-between,* where most of life happens. We cannot be perfect, our relationships are not perfect, and although we may love our jobs, some of our tasks are boring, and there are probably days that are stressful. When we change our thinking to be more reality-based, we will be more grateful for the positives that we do experience.

Our minds were created to work *for* us rather than against us. Once we become aware of our faulty thinking, we have the power to change the way we think. When we catch ourselves falling into one of these faulty thinking traps, we need to STOP and take a moment to review our thoughts. The next step is to replace the error with a rational, more positive, or less limiting thought. We are often our own stumbling block by the way that we think. Our challenge is to *get out of our own way* by thinking more rationally.

My faulty thinking is usually about…
I can correct my faulty thinking by…
My clear, rational thoughts are:

Negative thinking and self-talk

We create our life experience by our thoughts, words, and actions. Negative thinking creates negative experiences. Positive thinking creates positive experiences. If we want to change our life to be less difficult and more satisfying, we must first change our thoughts. We will not be successful in creating and maintaining healthy self-esteem if we are critical, disrespectful, and have little compassion and understanding for ourselves.

Our negative thoughts, which are based in fear and insecurities, may include losing relationships and being alone, what people think, what people say, how people have harmed us, and that life is a series of problems. Fear and worry thoughts, contrary to what some people think, do not prevent difficult situations. Because we are focusing our energy on the negative possibilities, we increase the probability of them happening. A persistent pattern of negative thinking becomes a habit, and like any other habit, it is difficult to break. When we have an unwillingness to change our negative ways of thinking, we continue to use unhealthy patterns of thought, which keeps us in our self-created mental bondage. When challenged to choose more positive thoughts, we may decline because we think that change would be too difficult and it wouldn't make any difference anyway.

Self-talk

Self-talk is the monologue within our minds that is usually not in our conscious awareness. Self-talk is our stream of thoughts as we evaluate the things we see, hear, and do, which may be positive or negative. When we observe others, we may think and say to ourselves, "I really like his shirt," or "She has beautiful blue eyes," or "He is so self-centered," or "She is so condescending and irritating!" We also evaluate ourselves regarding our words, actions, appearance, and competence. We may say to ourselves, "I think I did a good job with this situation!" Or, "I'm not good enough to sing in the choir!"

When our thoughts and self-talk are predominantly negative, it is because we have an overactive *inner critic,* which echoes the statements of critical parents and other dysfunctional people in our childhood, or people in our current lives who are unfairly critical in their efforts to control us. Our inner critic often criticizes how we look, what we say and how we say it, and tells us that we are not going to succeed at whatever we are doing. When our self-talk is orchestrated by our inner critic, we make self-negating statements such as, "I can't do it," "I'm not lovable," "I'm inadequate," "I'll never be a success," or, "I'm not good enough." Our thoughts and self-talk are fueled by our core beliefs about ourselves.

What we say to ourselves creates how we feel and what we do. We usually do not realize the profound effect our negative inner dialogue has on our life experience. Nor do we realize how powerful it is when our self-talk is positive, encouraging, respectful, and reflects a belief in our ability to meet the challenges of life. When our inner dialogue is saturated with negativity, we create a reality that is stressful, self-defeating, and is mentally, emotionally, physically, and spiritually unhealthy.

Examples of negative thoughts and self-talk:

- I'll never learn this computer program because I'm so dumb!
- Everybody takes advantage of me!
- I'm not good enough to get on the team!
- I'm a terrible employee, spouse, child, or parent. Or, the reverse—I have a terrible employer, spouse, child, or parent.
- I don't deserve to be loved.
- I don't deserve to take up space on the planet.

Our negative self-talk usually amplifies when we have made a mistake. The first step is tuning in and listening to our self-talk and becoming more aware of what we are saying to ourselves. When our self-talk is negative, we can visualize a stop sign and stop the thought. The next step is to identify how it is false, exaggerated, or distorted. We can then delete the thought from our mind and replace it with a more accurate or truthful thought. As we increasingly use positive self-talk and grow in self-esteem, our inner critic will lose its power over us.

Negative thoughts to delete	Positive thoughts
❖ I am stupid	I am intelligent
❖ I am inadequate	I am accomplishing my goals
❖ I'm unworthy	I am worthy
❖ There is something wrong with me	I am okay

Our physical bodies also respond to our self-talk. When our self-talk is repeatedly making statements such as "I always get a cold in the summer," or "I know I'm going to get a headache today" or, "I know this medication isn't going to do any good," our physical body can both hear and act on our words. It would be far better to have positive thoughts and self-talk such as, "Today I will experience perfect health!"

Our unhealthy ways of thinking need to be identified because they are life-diminishing and damaging to our self-esteem. When we correct our thinking errors, we are set free from the emotional pain and stress that we inadvertently create for ourselves. Research repeatedly confirms that the way we think affects our mental, emotional, spiritual, and physical health. When our thinking and self-talk predict negative events, our predictions often come true. In contrast, when we wake up and tell ourselves that it is going to be a great day, we are likely to experience what our minds are thinking and what our self-talk is saying. Our thinking and self-talk can become our ally, rather than an enemy that barrages us with negativity. Our goal is to have positive, encouraging, and affirming thoughts and self-talk, which will be beneficial to our whole life experience.

- Amber shares:

    I was negative so often, I didn't even realize I was negative. If I caught a cold, I knew it would be the worst cold ever. It was the same every time I got sick, and I got sick a lot. When people told me that I was negative, I thought they were just being mean and critical of me. But then I started losing a lot of my friends, and it seemed like nobody wanted to be around me. I started getting really depressed—like I could hardly function. And for some reason, I started thinking about my behaviors instead of everyone else's. I went to the book store and browsed around in the self-help section and found some information on depression and also negative thinking. Now I'm wondering how I fell into the trap of always being so dark, dreary, doom, and gloom.

My negative thoughts and self-talk are:

My new positive thoughts and self-talk:

❖ **Discarding irrational beliefs and toxic guilt**

Our irrational beliefs are usually not in our conscious awareness, but adversely affect our emotional lives and our relationships. As we become more aware of our irrational beliefs, we can identify why they are irrational and discard them. The following are some examples of common irrational beliefs that cause problems and lower our self-esteem:

- ✓ I should be able to do all things and do them perfectly.
- ✓ I cannot make mistakes; mistakes are bad and reveal just how incompetent I really am.
- ✓ I am inadequate and unworthy.
- ✓ I cannot create my own happiness.
- ✓ My value as a person is measured by my accomplishments and my social and financial status.
- ✓ I will always be abandoned.
- ✓ I am not good enough and don't deserve to be loved.
- ✓ Suffering is more virtuous than being happy.
- ✓ When bad things happen it is always my fault.
- ✓ I should be able to make decisions that are always right.

Most of us have irrational beliefs which influence our perceptions and feelings, and create internal stress.

What irrational beliefs need to be discarded so that I can recover, live fully, and grow in self-esteem?

I can replace my irrational beliefs with these positive and more accurate thoughts:

Irrational beliefs are the basis for *toxic guilt*

The feeling of guilt is the appropriate emotion when there is actual wrongdoing. In contrast, **toxic guilt** is feeling guilty when we have done nothing wrong and is based on an irrational belief. Besides creating toxic guilt for ourselves by our irrational thinking, we often accept the guilt that others project on us as a way to control us. Guilt that is rooted in irrational thinking is our foe because it is unfair and life-diminishing. However, guilt is our friend when it alerts us to actual wrongdoing and prompts us to make amends. (Rogne, C. *Anger and Guilt – Our Foes and Friends, 2011*).

Many examples of irrational guilt are provided in the following chart. We can recognize toxic guilt by clue words such as "should" or "always." We can trace each guilt feeling back to the irrational thought or belief.

Irrational guilt with *myself*   **Irrational thought or belief**

Irrational guilt with *myself*	Irrational thought or belief
Feeling guilty when I have been emotionally, physically, mentally, or sexually abused. Victims often take on the guilt that rightfully belongs to the perpetrator.	Irrational thought or belief: The abuse must have been my fault.
Feeling guilty when I am not God-like: all-knowing, all-loving, all-forgiving, and able to do all things perfectly.	Irrational thought or belief: I should be able to be all-knowing, all-loving, all-forgiving, and do all things perfectly.
Feeling guilty for confronting abusive behaviors appropriately, but the abuser feels emotionally hurt when faced with the truth.	Irrational thought or belief: I should never confront because I might hurt someone's feelings.

Feeling guilty when I'm not successful at removing others' emotional pain and making them happy.	Irrational thought or belief: I should be able to solve all problems and make people happy.
Feeling guilty for making mistakes, even if they are small and natural.	Irrational thought or belief: I cannot make mistakes because mistakes are bad and reveal just how incompetent I really am.
Feeling guilty because I am trying to respond to too many unrealistic expectations from others, am not always successful, and I become exhausted.	Irrational thought or belief: I should be able to successfully do all things for everyone, and others are more important than I am.
Feeling guilty because I am taking better care of myself, but now I feel like I am being selfish.	Irrational thought or belief: It is selfish to take care of myself.
Feeling guilty for being happy and positive when I am with people who are unhappy and negative.	Irrational thought or belief: I don't deserve to be happy, and I believe that suffering is more virtuous than being happy.
Feeling guilty for being angry, even though the anger is a response to being harmed.	Irrational thought or belief: I should never be angry.
Feeling guilty when saying "no!"	Irrational thought or belief: I am bad and selfish when I don't respond to everyone's requests.

Feeling guilty for not being attractive, handsome, slim, young, successful, intelligent, outgoing, a great cook, a great lover, a super dancer, a millionaire, the *perfect* wife, husband, friend, child, employer, employee, housecleaner, parent, athlete, or student.	Irrational thought or belief: I should be able to do all things perfectly, even the impossible.
Feeling guilty for having time conflicts, for working too much, for not working enough, for not exercising enough, for asking for help, and for receiving help when I ask for it.	Irrational thought or belief: I should be able to do all things, even the impossible, for everyone and do all things perfectly and never need help.
Feeling guilty when someone is overly kind or generous to me.	Irrational thought or belief: I do not deserve kindness from others.
Feeling guilty for not feeling guilty.	Irrational thought or belief: Feeling guilty is virtuous and I should feel guilty.

Irrational guilt in *relationships*   **Irrational thought or belief**

Feeling guilty when I don't meet all of my partner's needs and wants.	Irrational thought or belief: I should be able to meet all of my partner's needs and wants.
Feeling guilty when I express feelings that displease my partner.	Irrational thought or belief: I should never express feelings that upset my partner.

Feeling guilty for not wanting to be sexual.	Irrational thought or belief: I should always want to be sexual when my partner does.
Feeling guilty for needing meaningful communication in a significant relationship.	Irrational thought or belief: I should have no needs in my relationships.

Irrational guilt with *parents*   **Irrational thought or belief**

Feeling guilty because I never felt loved and couldn't make my parents love me.	Irrational thought or belief: I should have been able to make my parents love me.
Feeling guilty because when I was a child, I could not rescue myself or my family members from abuse.	Irrational thought or belief: Even though I was a child, I should have been able to rescue myself and family members from any type of abuse.
Feeling guilty when thinking that I'm not living up to my parents' expectations.	Irrational thought or belief: I should always live up to my parents' expectations, even the expectations I create in my mind that may not be true.

Irrational guilt with *children*	**Irrational thought or belief**
Feeling guilty when my children make mistakes or misbehave.	Irrational thought or belief: If my children fail in any way, it's my fault.
Feeling guilty when I don't buy whatever my children want.	Irrational thought or belief: I should give my children everything that I didn't have as a child.
Feeling guilty when I take time to exercise, go to a support group, or have coffee with friends.	Irrational thought or belief: I don't deserve to take care of myself or relax.
Feeling guilty for not working outside of the home but also feeling guilty if working outside of the home.	Irrational thought or belief: I should not work so that I can be with my children, but I should work outside of the home to earn an income.

Rational thoughts to correct irrational thoughts that lead to feeling guilty

- We are not God. We have limited powers and wisdom.
- We cannot correct a problem that is beyond our power, competency, and authority, or when we do not have the power to positively impact all of the reasons that create the problem.
- Doing our best is important, but we do not have to be perfect.
- It is not selfish to invest energies into taking care of ourselves.
- We cannot change other persons' behaviors or take away

their pain. We can support their efforts toward healing and growth, but we can't do it for them.
- We have a right to refuse to be the one who does most of the physical work, as well as the emotional work, such as nurturing or communicating in a relationship.
- We have a right to confront a person who is emotionally abusing us by controlling us with anger, badgering us into submission, or trying to make us feel guilty.
- We can choose to leave an abusive, toxic relationship that is unlikely to change and not feel guilty. We can leave by emotionally detaching or physically removing ourselves and our children.
- We do not have to feel guilty when we do not want to be sexual with our partner. We have a right to make choices about our physical body.
- We do not have to feel guilty for needing emotional intimacy in a primary relationship.
- If we express our anger appropriately and it is legitimate, we do not have to feel guilty.
- We do not have to feel guilty if we have different interests, values, and priorities than our spouse or friends.

- Melissa shares:

    My name is Melissa and I am the true Queen of guilt. The only reason I can joke about this is that I see it now and have learned to stop thinking in ways that make myself feel guilty and miserable. I have been the guilty daughter, spouse, and mother. I feel guilty when I work outside the home and feel guilty when I stay at home with my children. Every time I spend money, I feel guilty, and if I spend money just for something fun, I really feel guilty. I feel guilty when I can't please my mother, even though I know that it is impossible to please mom. I feel guilty when I can't get to all of my children's school programs and when I pick up fast food for supper. I feel guilty when I go to church because I am told I am a sinner, and I feel guilty if I don't go to church. So now I am trying to get rid of my garbage bag of guilt—not the guilt where I really mess up, but the guilt that I create with my mind. It feels good! I am getting rid of the shackles around my feet that keep me stuck.

Steps to deal with *irrational* guilt

Changing our irrational beliefs that create toxic guilt involves the following process:

1. Identify the irrational belief that is causing irrational guilt.
2. Challenge the belief:
   - ✓ Is there any evidence that this belief is true?
   - ✓ Does this belief have words such as "never" or "always" or "should"? If so, it is probably irrational, exaggerated, or false.
   - ✓ Is this belief life-fostering or life-diminishing?
   - ✓ Is this belief fear-based?
3. If the belief and the guilt are determined to be irrational and life-diminishing, dismiss them.
4. Create a realistic belief to replace the irrational belief.
5. Continue life with the new belief. When you become aware of other irrational beliefs or irrational guilt, use this same process. If you are diligent in confronting irrational beliefs and toxic guilt, you will discover that the frequency of your irrational beliefs decreases, which means you are creating less stress, emotional pain, and guilt for yourself.

◄ Self-Esteem

> In the past, my unhealthy ways of dealing with guilt were:
>
> What irrational guilt am I carrying?
>
> What is the underlying irrational thought?
>
> What is a rational, logical thought?
>
> The guilt I have regarding my relationship is:
>
> What guilt can I dismiss?
>
> Dealing with guilt in healthy ways, I expect to feel:

Positive statements are helpful in replacing guilt-making, irrational beliefs

We can use positive statements to replace irrational thoughts that create toxic guilt. Writing and repeating our own positive statements can help us to reprogram our minds. Examples follow:

❖ I am able to identify the irrational though when I feel irrational guilt.

- ❖ I have no need to punish myself with guilt.
- ❖ I can do my best but do not have to be perfect to be successful or happy.
- ❖ I do not need to be all-knowing to be a good person.
- ❖ I release my irrational guilt because it serves no healthy purpose for me.
- ❖ I am discarding any thought or belief that is life-diminishing.

Since we live with ourselves our whole lifetime, a positive relationship with ourselves is crucial if we are to live up to our potential, have purpose in our lives, and have meaningful relationships. If we are healing from our childhood wounds, continuing in recovery for our addictions, and changing our faulty ways of thinking—which eliminates much of our toxic guilt— we are doing well in our recovery from low self-esteem. We are realizing that we *are* worthy, capable, and have infinite value. Our old belief that "There is something wrong with me" is losing its power over us.

> **Whether it involves our mental, emotional, physical, or spiritual selves, we have to *revise or discard whatever is life-diminishing, false, and negative* that adversely influences our lives and our self-esteem. These include addictions, negative learning about ourselves, faulty ways of thinking, irrational beliefs, and toxic guilt. When we are successful in discarding whatever is life-diminishing, we enhance our self-esteem and are more able to respect, value, embrace and appreciate ourselves.**

Chapter 7

Empowerment Strategies

*Remember always that you not only have a right to
be an individual, you have an obligation to be one.*
—Eleanor Roosevelt, advocate for civil rights

The controlling people in our lives may be spouses, ex-spouses, siblings, children, in-laws, dating partners, friends, neighbors, and/or colleagues. We may also feel controlled by dominant groups in society, and oppressive government, economic, religious, and political systems. The two most common forms of control are expressing anger aggressively and projecting guilt onto others. Since controllers' behaviors are unlikely to change, it is the recipients of control who need to be empowered in order to change power inequities.

If we have sufficient personal power, we may be able to confront controlling behaviors directed toward us. If it is not physically or emotionally safe to confront, we may be able to do less enabling of controlling behaviors. If we cannot stop enabling, because of possible consequences, we can know that having less power is not because we are innately inferior. The real reason is that power is often used in abusive and controlling ways to maintain self-serving benefits at the expense of less powerful people. This realization is empowering, even though we may not be able to change the power inequities.

❖ Empowering strategies when we are controlled

1. Claim your personal power

> *The most common way people give up*
> *their power is thinking they don't have any.*
> —Alice Walker, author, poet, activist

As adults, we have varying degrees of personal power, which may be different in our various roles as spouse, parent, employer, employee, or colleague. Empowering ourselves requires that we claim our power and become more aware of how we unknowingly give our power away. Some of us hesitate to explore power because of how power has been used against us, which left us with a belief that all power is abusive. However, power can be used in very positive ways to empower people through educating, supporting, and challenging.

We may feel powerless because a) controllers are orchestrating our life by their expectations and demands; b) we have internalized the negative statements made by a controller; or c) we have been influenced by cultural conditioning. However, many of us *have more power* than we think we have in our American culture. But our personal power is not going to be given or returned to us, nor are we going to be reminded that we do, in fact, have personal power. Claiming our power involves taking charge of ourselves and our lives. Though we may feel powerless, we must start believing that we have personal power and raising our awareness as to the many ways we give our power away.

Claiming our power involves:

- Focusing on our own behaviors: how *we* are responding to the controller, rather than focusing on the controller
- Knowing that we are not always at fault
- Refusing to listen to badgering, negative comments and derogatory labels, whether in person or on the phone, and deleting abusive text messages, unless they need to be saved for a police investigation
- Not changing our mood because of what a controller says or does
- Refusing to adjust our thoughts, values, beliefs, and actions to fit the controller's expectations or directives
- Refusing to get hooked into useless arguments
- Not providing information that may be twisted and used against us
- Refusing to make excuses for, rescue, take responsibility for, or suffer the consequences resulting from controllers' inappropriate behaviors
- Refusing to apologize when there is no valid reason to apologize
- Refusing to be a puppet, servant, the *parent,* or the *child* in our relationship
- Refusing to ask permission to do the things we want to do, as if we were children
- Emotionally detaching so that we do not harbor anger and resentment toward our controller, which are emotions that can compromise our health
- Refusing to stay in the victim role, which results in emotional, physical, spiritual, or mental collapse
- Refusing to believe that there is something innately wrong with us
- Refusing to support controlling behaviors by enabling, allowing, accommodating, adjusting, complying, protecting, sacrificing preferences and dreams, and pretending that

everything is fine when everything is not fine in order to be loved and prevent conflict

By claiming our power, in a number of ways and in different situations, we are being proactive and competent in managing our lives, which is a positive and powerful step in enhancing our self-esteem.

> I give my power away to the following persons:
>
> My plan for claiming my power:

2. Stay credible

Being credible requires being honest and living life with integrity so that what we say is what we do. We take responsibility for our actions, are emotionally balanced and are respectful to ourselves and others. If we are viewed as credible by controllers, we may avoid being their target and they may even distance themselves from us. Or, unfortunately, they will increase their control and relentlessly attempt to hurt or destroy us in a variety of ways. This is when it is even more crucial to stay credible.

When we are challenged by controlling behaviors, we cannot have angry outbursts, nor can we emotionally break down and cry if our intention is to stay credible. When we lose control of our behaviors, we will be discredited and dismissed as unstable and out of control. It often does not play out the same way for controllers. When controllers are abusive with their anger, they seldom take responsibility. They usually blame others and are not held accountable for their inappropriate communication or behaviors.

More powerful people often *define* a less powerful person or a person they want to discredit by *one incident.* For example, if a woman's voice starts to sound angry, or she is actually expressing anger, she is often labeled an angry woman. The incident defines her, is shared with others, and frequently becomes her reputation. In contrast, anger is often a symbol of power for men, and an inappropriate angry incident is often treated as an *exception.* Excuses are offered, and frequently, the people who make excuses for men's inappropriate behaviors are women.

Staying credible requires speaking in normal, pleasant, but firm voice tones in all of our interactions, but especially with controllers, whether they are a spouse, mother, father, child, or employer. By presenting ourselves in a credible and confident manner, we are more likely to be taken seriously and will not be giving our controllers a reason to discredit what we are saying.

Ways that I can be credible are:

My current challenges with controllers are:

---

2. Be assertive

If we are passive, we are not respectful of ourselves. When we are aggressive, we are not respectful of others. Assertiveness is being respectful and honest to both ourselves and others.

Passive Behaviors	Assertive Behaviors	Aggressive Behaviors
Are not respectful of self: I am inferior, you are superior	*Are respectful to both self and others: we are both equal, and neither one of us is inferior*	*Are not respectful of others: I am superior, you are inferior*
➤ Not expressing anger ➤ Disrespectful of self ➤ Blaming of self ➤ Being dishonest with feelings ➤ Being indirect ➤ Seemingly content to lose ➤ Not self-advocating ➤ Not asking directly for help ➤ Letting people invade personal boundaries ➤ Trying to please everyone at one's own expense	➤ Expressing anger appropriately ➤ Respecting others ➤ Respecting the self ➤ Being honest and direct ➤ Self-advocating ➤ Addressing difficult issues and feelings ➤ Using "I" messages ➤ Asking directly for help ➤ Staying within one's own personal boundaries ➤ Able to protect one's own boundaries	➤ Expressing anger aggressively ➤ Taking a superior position to gain an advantage ➤ Disrespecting others ➤ Dominating, threatening, or intimidating others with anger ➤ Ordering or commanding ➤ Invading others' boundaries ➤ Blaming others ➤ Being dishonest ➤ Attempting to win at the other's expense or sacrifice

It is impossible to effectively problem-solve when a controlling person is using *one-up* tactics to win. Nor does it work to negotiate changes when someone takes a *one-down* position and poses as helpless. Effective problem-solving occurs when all persons are honest and assertive. In the assertive position, people have equal status. No one takes a *one-up* or *one-down* position. There is mutual respect and valuing of others' opinions.

Being assertive when confronting

- Set a time and place to speak to the person.
- Rehearse in your mind or write down what needs to be said. You can also think about possible responses by the controller and mentally prepare assertive responses in return.
- Start sentences with "I," rather than "You," to avoid blaming statements.
- Use short sentences when confronting.
- Speak with truthfulness, firmness, respectfulness, kindness, and in normal voices tones.
- Listen as well as speak.
- Speak directly about the behavior that is offensive to you rather than expecting the person to *get the drift*.
- Resist the temptation to end the conversation because of emotional discomfort.
- Stick to the specifics of the current situation rather than bringing up past hurts.
- Repeat the original statement if the other person becomes defensive, starts discounting what is being said, or changes the topic.
- Go slowly and pay attention to what is happening in the communication process.
- Take a time-out if there is the possibility of an eruption of anger.
- Practice calming inner self-talk.
- Being assertive also means affirming others. Affirm the

person for listening and having the willingness to address the issues causing the conflict.

> In what situations in my life do I need to become more assertive?
>
> How will I accomplish this?

3. Counteract *one-up, one-down control tactics*

To develop a strategy to handle *one-up, one-down* tactics, we need to review this behavior. Being critical, taking over conversations, or making demands are ways of taking a *one-up* position. Controllers often say, "You shouldn't feel that way," which is a statement that discounts a victim's feelings, and is an attempt to put the person in a *one-down*, powerless and passive position. Saying that a person shouldn't feel a certain way sends the message that if the person feels hurt, offended, or angry, the person is wrong and inadequate. This takes the responsibility off of the perpetrator and places it on the victim, rather than the controller taking responsibility for the harm that was done. The perpetrator stays *one-up,* and the victim is put in a *one-down* position. If a person stays alert to the communication of controllers, many *one-up* and *one-down* statements can be identified.

Taking a *one-up* position ranges from making sarcastic comments to serious verbal attacks. In contrast, a controller might take a *one-down* position, especially *when a one-up position is not successful* at getting compliance. This is posturing as being helpless or victimized and using guilt in efforts to control another person. The unspoken message of most guilt trips is that the person being manipulated does not care enough, is selfish and inconsiderate. Persons respond out of obligation rather than choice.

While controllers continue their *one-up, one-down* tactics, they are usually not aware that there is a neutral, middle, assertive position, which is increasingly being understood and utilized by people who refuse to be manipulated and is neither a *one-up* nor a *one-down* position. When someone holds firm in a neutral position, rather than being manipulated by a *one-up* or *one-down* statement, controllers are often unsure of what to do because their control maneuvers are not working.

If we are certain that we will be physically safe when confronting a controller, we can counteract the *one-up, one-down* controlling tactics. Repeating our original statement, which is not said in an aggressive way or a passive, *one-down* way, is the best strategy when communicating with a controller. If a controller tries to put us down in order to take a superior position, we do not have to take a *one-down* position. We can self-advocate, be assertive, and speak in a credible way to the controller. If the controller takes a *one-down* position and tries to impose guilt on us, again, we do not have to accept the guilt. We can once again be assertive and speak in a credible way.

The following is a *one-up, one-down* scenario:

Controller A: "You are overreacting!" (This is a *one-up* statement to establish a superior, *one-up* position by assigning blame to the other person.)

Person B: "I am not overreacting. Your behavior is unacceptable." (This is an assertive statement. Person B is not manipulated into a *one-down* position.)

Controller A: "Unacceptable! What is that supposed to mean?" (Another *one-up* statement. The unspoken message is that Person B is exaggerating and way off base.)

Person B: "I am not overreacting. Your behavior is unacceptable." (Person B is taking an assertive position and repeating what was previously said.)

Controller A: "Well, I guess I must be a really bad person!" (This is a *one-down* statement, meant to manipulate Person B to retract the statement. If the person retracts, Controller A resumes the *one-up* position.)

Person B: "Your behavior is unacceptable." (Person B does not retract the statement.)

The outcome of this communication is that the controller did not succeed in putting Person B in a *one-down* position. Person B did not give away his/her power and was not manipulated by Controller A.

4. Protect your personal boundaries

Personal boundaries are our physical, mental, and emotional limits that distinguish and separate us from other people. We have a right to our personal space, and to be mentally, emotionally, sexually, and physically safe in our relationships. Most persons in our culture are able to manage their boundaries unless there is a potential for violence, which is always invasive and devastating to personal boundaries.

Controlling people are often disrespectful of personal boundaries. They invade personal space and often act entitled to the mental, emotional, social, sexual, and physical life of another. When we struggle with low self-esteem, we often let others violate our boundaries. As a result, we are often told what we should do, think, feel, or experience. It is unlikely that controllers will willingly function within their own boundaries. Therefore, the victims of boundary breakers need to learn how to defend their boundaries.

People who have healthy personal boundaries:

- ✓ Are able to say "no" when necessary
- ✓ Do not accept verbal, emotional, or physical abuse from others
- ✓ Readily confront boundary breakers
- ✓ Decide what is true, rather than automatically internalizing criticisms
- ✓ Have assertiveness skills and are able to self-advocate
- ✓ Have healthy self-esteem
- ✓ Are respectful of others' boundaries

We have a right and responsibility to set limits on what is unacceptable behavior directed toward us. If we struggle with low self-esteem, strengthening our personal boundaries may be difficult. We have to understand and believe that we have a right to personal boundaries. It is our way of communicating to others that we have self-respect, self-worth, and self-confidence.

Situation:	My plan to protect my personal boundaries:

5. Know your personal rights in relationships

If we are in a controlling relationship, we probably need to be reminded that *we have basic rights* in relationships. Controllers frequently trample on the rights of others and often steal the energy and joy from their partners. The following is a summary of the basic rights we should have in relationships.

We have a right to:

- Live free from emotional, physical, or sexual abuse
- Confront when being unjustly criticized or falsely blamed
- Be treated as an equal, with respect, honesty, and fairness
- Be taken seriously
- Share in decision making
- Talk freely about troubling situations
- Be free from control and pressure
- Receive clear and informative answers to questions
- Be respectfully asked rather than ordered
- Refuse requests
- Have our own opinion and change our mind if necessary
- Make our own decisions about our life
- Communicate openly
- Have privacy
- Choose what we do with our body
- Express our feelings and emotions
- Have other healthy friendships and participate in activities of interest without being criticized
- Believe in ourselves and feel good about who we are

Knowing our rights is empowering, and having our rights respected draws us closer to our partner, parent, friend, or colleague. However, when people trample on any of these rights, we have a legitimate reason to confront them in an appropriate and credible manner.

> What rights do I need to defend?
>
> How will I do this?

6. Self-advocate

Self-advocacy is speaking up for ourselves and asking questions when we need information. With healthy self-esteem, we are more able and willing to self-advocate, even though it may be easier to remain quiet. Perhaps the most difficult part of self-advocating is using refusal skills so that we are able to make statements such as "No," or "Not now, but I could do it later," or, "I have plans, so I can't do that." At the end of a sentence, we need to speak in a voice tone that indicates closure, and conveys that there is nothing more to talk about. It may be a challenge for us to communicate these simple statements without taking them back, apologizing for saying them, or feeling guilty because the controlling person's feelings are hurt when faced with the truth.

Advocating for ourselves is likely to be viewed by a controller as being uncooperative and selfish. If we suspect that these accusations will be made, we can be prepared for such statements. We can refuse to internalize the unfair criticisms and decide whether to ignore or confront the statements. Some statements are so off base, false, and manipulative that they are not worthy of being acknowledged.

> I need to self-advocate when:
>
> The difficult part of self-advocating is:

7. Do less enabling

Enabling is helping the controller to be successful in their controlling behaviors. It is like buying alcohol for the alcoholic, calling their workplace to report their illness when it is actually a hangover, and cleaning up their messes. Enabling allows others to avoid the consequences of dysfunctional and abusive actions. When we enable, we allow, accommodate, adjust, comply, protect, sacrifice preferences and dreams, and pretend that everything is fine when everything is not fine.

People comply with and enable controlling behaviors for many reasons, such as preventing conflict, staying employed, being financially able to sustain themselves and their families, to be loved, and to protect themselves and their children. Many of us comply with controllers' demands because we don't want to be viewed as someone who creates hassles, or is mean, selfish, and uncaring.

Enabling stems from good intentions, but results in fueling the controlling behaviors. There are some controlling situations where it is impossible to stop enabling because the consequences may be too high, such as increased control, the threat of violence, or actual physical abuse. However, every time we enable, we sacrifice our honesty, respect for ourselves, and self-esteem.

Enabling is:

- ✓ Being silent so we don't create a hassle
- ✓ Going along to get along, even though agreeing might conflict with personal values
- ✓ Trying to meet the controller's numerous expectations
- ✓ Not being honest to prevent conflict
- ✓ Failing to set limits on what is acceptable and what is not acceptable
- ✓ Internalizing the controller's guilt statements and acting out of obligation
- ✓ Trying to be, do, think, feel, and behave according to what the controller wants rather than being true to ourselves
- ✓ Changing personal preferences and interests to match the controller's preferences and interests
- ✓ Praising the controller's positive behaviors that should be expected in relationships, such as saying, "Thank you for being nice to me."
- ✓ Being compliant, passive, and not standing up for what we believe in efforts to prevent, avoid, or stop a hassle
- ✓ Laughing at inappropriate and offensive humor
- ✓ Trying to do things perfectly to avoid criticism and anger
- ✓ Agreeing when we really disagree
- ✓ Agreeing to participate in disliked or uninteresting activities
- ✓ Not talking about anything controversial
- ✓ Hiding emotional pain
- ✓ Minimizing the emotional damage that is being created by dysfunction
- ✓ Confronting the controlling behavior but then retracting what is said
- ✓ Placing more important on the controllers' preferences, interests, goals, and dreams than our own

- ✓ Not actualizing our own life regarding our work or personal development to prevent conflict in a relationship
- ✓ Crying but insisting that nothing is wrong
- ✓ Pretending to be okay when in emotional pain
- ✓ Saying that we are not angry when we *are* angry

Enabling dysfunctional or controlling behaviors may have begun in childhood to avoid conflict with parents. We continue to enable in adulthood, often at the expense of our honesty, emotions, money, personal time, and self-esteem.

We are more likely to enable when we believe that we do not have the option to *exit* a relationship. Usually, the key issues regarding a divorce decision are a) safety, b) the effects on children, and c) financial resources. This brings to the forefront the importance of directing efforts into becoming self-sustaining from young adulthood. Financial resources provide options in life, including leaving a toxic relationship or job. We are less likely to enable or remain in an abusive relationship if we can financially afford to leave. With sufficient financial resources we can also make the divorce transition less traumatic for ourselves and our children. We may be able to keep them in their same home, school, and activities, continue to provide learning opportunities for them, and avoid working overtime or two jobs to support the family. There is less stress when there is not everyday financial pressure, which children are sure to feel. In contrast, there are people who are controlled to the point of deciding that, regardless of what happens to them financially, they will leave and survive in some way. When we are this desperate, the leaving process can be very traumatic for every member of the family.

◄ Self-Esteem

> In what ways do I enable dysfunctional behaviors?
>
> What enabling can I stop doing?
>
> How will I feel when I do less enabling?

8. Plan, rehearse, and confront

Rather than enabling controlling behaviors, we need to confront, if we know we will be physically safe. Planning what we need to say helps us to keep focused and maintain self-control. We can write everything we would like to say and edit our writing until it is exactly what we want to communicate. We need to be specific when talking to our controller about the mental or emotional abuse. It is important to make it clear what we will no longer tolerate. When the conversation is emotionally difficult, it is helpful to keep the interaction short. Clearly state what will not be tolerated with statements such as, "I am no longer going to be quiet when your controlling behaviors are affecting the children," or, "I will talk to you as soon as you settle down," or, "I am no longer going to be worried about hurting *your* feelings when I confront your verbal abuse." It is likely that the controller will have a rebuttal to these statements or he/she may become upset, make excuses, minimize or deny the problem. The best strategy is to repeat the original statement in normal voice tones. Even if you think that the conversation won't change the controller's behaviors, at least you have advocated for yourself rather than being a passive recipient of the abuse, whatever form it took.

> Who do I need to confront?
>
> I need to say or write:

9. Provide less information

Providing too much information is a common behavior of people who feel powerless when relating to a controller. When we provide too many details, it sounds as if we have done something wrong. We can usually determine whether a person's questions are out of concern and caring, or whether the questions are out of a need to control. When asked by a controller, "Where have you been?" we often explain at length why we needed to go someplace, what time we started, why we chose this particular day, how we used our time, who we were with, and why it took so long. Rather than going into a long explanation of our activities, we can make short statements, such as "I was doing errands." If our controller interrogates us or makes a sarcastic comment such as "I suppose you had a great time without me," we can respond with "yes," or "no," or "whatever," or offer no response. We can convey in kind and short sentences that we are responsible adults who do not need a controller to tell us what to do. Controllers' behaviors are attempts to feel superior, but if we refuse to play their mind games, controllers are disarmed.

◄ Self-Esteem

> My plan for giving less information when I am questioned by a controller:

10. Apologize when harm has been done to others

We need to apologize for actual wrongdoing that has been harmful to others. But making false apologies when we have done nothing wrong is a form of dishonesty because our actions have not actually hurt others. Saying "I'm sorry" after we have confronted a controller's inappropriate behaviors, or being apologetic when spending money for the family groceries or visiting a sick parent, are apologies that imply that we have done something wrong. These types of apologies come from a passive, powerless position and are often done to smooth over a relationship problem or pacify a controller. There may be other reasons for apologizing for no reason, but each time we engage in this behavior, our self-esteem suffers.

> The last time I apologized for no reason was…
>
> My motivation was…

11. Consider relationship options

When physical, emotional, or mental abuse continues in a relationship, even though we have confronted in assertive and credible ways, we may think we have no options. Sometimes we think that we should try longer and harder, despite a history of unsuccessful efforts. During other days, leaving the relationship seems to be the only option. Each of the following options poses a challenge and a risk. Most often, we are emotionally and mentally weaving in and out of more than one of these options when we are involved in an emotionally and mentally abusive relationship.

- **Option # 1: remain in the emotional pain**

This is not a good option, but it *is* an option and is usually a choice we make by *not* making a choice. Staying in emotional pain is risky because we do not always recognize our increasing vulnerability and dysfunction. Choosing this option may result in behaviors such as overworking, avoiding going home, getting involved in another relationship, or using alcohol, drugs, or addictive activities to cope with the emotional pain and emptiness of an oppressive and deteriorating relationship. Remaining in emotional pain eventually leads to depression. Not only does depression create emotional darkness and hopelessness, but it also numbs our feelings, including our anger, which is the emotion that is often needed to motivate ourselves to make changes. Option # 1 presents a risk because we may become exhausted from emotional pain or from the activities we are doing to alleviate the pain and emptiness. We may become entrapped by an addiction that controls our life. We cannot remain in this option for long periods of time if we are going to take care of ourselves and our children.

- **Option # 2: emotionally detach from the relationship**

If our strategies for dealing with our controller fall on deaf ears and the controlling behaviors persist, we need to emotionally detach. Disengagement or detachment is not abandonment of the dysfunctional person. Rather, it is refusing to be manipulated by controlling statements and behaviors or have our moods and daily experiences adversely affected. When we detach, we can create a life that is more emotionally separated from the dysfunctional person but connected to whatever degree is necessary to co-exist and co-parent children.

By detaching, we no longer allow the dysfunctional person to create high levels of stress and anxiety in our lives, nor do we enable controlling behaviors. We refuse to sacrifice our choices as to how we use our time, what we do, or whom we associate with in order to prevent conflict with a dysfunctional person. We stop being a hostage to whomever or whatever is controlling us. In essence, we *get a life,* and live our lives according to *our* design.

Enabling dysfunctional behaviors is actually a *disservice* not only to ourselves but to dysfunctional people. If we contribute to the success of dysfunctional behaviors, there will be no motivation to change. When we detach and stop enabling, we are using *tough love*, which is caring enough to no longer enable behaviors that are harmful to the person we care about, to ourselves, and to our children. Though we may not be able to stop the dysfunction, we create a higher probability for behaviors to change because the behaviors are not enabled; therefore, they are less successful. If the dysfunctional behaviors do not stop, we know that the behaviors we experience today will be the same behaviors we will experience in one year, five years, or twenty. This is vital information that we need in making decisions about an abusive or non-functional relationship.

Detachment is:

- Emotionally disconnecting from another's unhealthy behaviors
- Not giving away our personal power
- Not enabling unacceptable behaviors
- Refusing to get hooked into a dysfunctional person's emotional turmoil and negativity
- Refusing to have moods, thoughts, choices, or plans change because of a controller
- Refusing to internalize unjust criticisms and act out of fear, insecurity, or limitation
- Refusing to believe that taking care of the self and setting personal limits are selfish behaviors
- Letting dysfunctional people clean up their own messes, fixing their relationship problems with children, friends, colleagues, or parents; and finding their own ways to sustain themselves financially.

Detaching is emotionally stepping out of the circle of drama and control. When we detach, we take care of ourselves and honor the life that has been given to us. If we plan to stay in a dysfunctional, controlling relationship and stay healthy ourselves, detaching is crucial. Detaching is difficult because we are accustomed to allowing and enabling the dysfunctional behaviors. Emotionally detaching from a dysfunctional person is not a total solution but does reduce the stress of getting caught up in the dysfunction.

Whether a spouse or significant other does or does not abuse chemicals, dysfunctional and controlling people display many alcoholic behaviors such as blaming others, being aggressively angry, being demanding, being dishonest, and living in denial. The Al-Anon Twelve-Step Program teaches the basic principles of detachment and living a life based on spiritual and mental health principles. People are emotionally supported in Al-Anon groups and empower each other. This has literally saved the emotional lives of thousands of people who are involved with a controller whose behavior is the same as alcoholic or dry-drunk behaviors.

- **Option # 3: leave the relationship**

This is a very difficult choice when there are children. If safety is involved, children need to be removed from danger. If there is constant arguing and yelling and children are cowering in their bedrooms out of fear, the children need to be removed from the abuse and provided with an environment that is physically, mentally, and emotionally safe.

Working with a therapist or participating in a support group is helpful when making a divorce decision. We need to thoughtfully consider the many factors that are involved in our decision and also carefully plan the steps of the leaving process so that there is less trauma for all involved. Some adults are angry at their non-abusing parent for not removing them from the controller's dysfunction when they were children. In contrast to taking no action, some parents say, "My dysfunctional partner controlled me, but when it started to affect the children, I mustered up the courage and strength to leave."

- Mary shares:

    I was miserably unhappy in a controlling relationship, but I did my best to keep it going, for the sake of the kids. I didn't want them to live in two homes. So I became unhealthier, felt more stressed, enabled his controlling behaviors to try to prevent conflict, tried to keep the peace, and stuffed my feelings. Not a good place to be. Sometimes I could forget about how miserable I was because I loved my children and enjoyed being with them. I also liked my job. So quite often, I could put my relationship aside. And sometimes I would be overwhelmed with sadness, feeling inferior, feeling at fault, and feeling inadequate, which were all of the things that my spouse told me that I came to accept as truth.

> What option am I currently in?
>
> If this option is not working, what is my next step?

12. Reject harmful, controlling stereotypes

Men's stereotypes are to be strong, productive, athletic, unemotional, independent, competitive, and aggressive. Typical cultural directives for women include expectations to make adjustments; accommodate and please others; be meek, adaptable, compliant, nice, and attractive. If people have characteristics, values, and priorities contrary to stereotypical expectations, they are viewed as different, even inferior. However, many of the stereotypes for both women are contrary to the principles of mental health.

Many men believe that sharing feelings is a sign of weakness, rather than being emotionally, physically, and spiritual healthy. They are discouraged from showing basic human qualities that provide meaning in life, such as nurturing others, being honest and open with their emotions, and extending themselves to others in compassionate ways. More men are realizing that they can reject male stereotypes. They are enjoying their nurturing abilities and are taking an active role in parenting.

◄ Self-Esteem

- Tim shares:

    I was never very athletic growing up and sometimes the other boys would tease me, especially in junior high, about being a wimp, gay or that I was weird. I could get along with the girls, but other than a couple of guy-friends, I was pretty much a loner. What changed my life was taking golf lessons, and I really enjoyed golf. Because I felt good about golfing, I spent a lot of time on the golf course. Guys didn't give me a bad time. They respected me because of how well I golfed, so I just kept it up, all through high school and college. Even now when I have some extra time, I will head for the golf course. Golf really took away the feelings of being inadequate because I was not macho, big and strong like many of the other guys. So I am lucky to have picked up that first golf club because I started feeling a lot better about myself.

Typical cultural directives for women encourage them to believe and act like they are powerless, passive, and people-pleasing. If they are assertive, they are often considered to be aggressive and are labeled with derogatory names. When they disagree, they are called stubborn and uncooperative.

- Kelly shares:

    I have spent a fortune on staying thin, being gorgeous and hanging out with the right people, who lived in big homes, in the exclusive section of town. It worries me that I will not be accepted, so I spend a lot of time on my appearance. If I didn't put on my makeup and dress well, I know I would meet someone in the grocery store that would see me for who I really am, and that would not be cool. Money is no issue. My husband's company is very successful, so I don't have anything to worry about, except him meeting someone else who is more attractive or more interesting. It probably sounds like I shouldn't have any problems and that I have the American dream life. But I'm not very happy. I probably drink too much alcohol, but I don't drink any more than my friends. There are a lot of parties, and if you don't go to the parties, they talk about you. Every once in a while, I think about how I have really followed the *rules* as far as being a female, but I'm not sure I like where it has taken me. I feel empty and I don't know where my life is going, but shopping always helps when I have these thoughts.

Many stereotypical directives are contrary to being emotionally, physically, and spiritually healthy. Unless we have awareness of the false premises in stereotypes, we may feel inferior, different, broken, or wrong if we are unable or unwilling to pattern our thoughts, attitudes, and behaviors to match cultural stereotypes. When this is our experience, we frequently conclude that "There is something wrong with me," and our self-esteem suffers.

With growing awareness, we can dismiss stereotypes as cultural directives that we do not have to follow. They are only constructs that frequently support those in power. We can be our own individual person with unique characteristics. If we are living with positive principles, we need not apologize or feel inferior if we do not conform to stereotypes. In fact, we are likely to be healthier if we distance ourselves completely from their influence.

> What stereotypes can I reject because they are life-diminishing?

13. Direct your life by your own values

Peer pressure did not stop in adolescence. It only became more subtle. If we succumb to the control and influence of a materialistic society, we will get caught up in frenzied activity, distracting ourselves with entertainment, accumulating possessions, doing whatever is necessary to be with the popular crowd, spending excessive time in our addictions, and viewing media productions that are forgotten the next day. A lot of time and money are spent on creating a good outside appearance. Financial problems often arise when people pose as being more affluent than they really are, in efforts to have others view them as having a high social status, which is often equated with being a person having value. There is a considerable amount of emotional dishonesty. Though some people say that their spouse and children are the most important to them, they actually spend little time with them. Following the crowd and going along with the trends of a materialistic society will eventually leave us emotionally and spiritually empty. We have all read about or know people who have wealth, fame, and endless luxuries, but are restless, irritable, and discontent.

Although our society discourages going within, finding our own answers, discovering our strengths, and living a spiritual life, there are no actual barriers to choosing this path. We can reject what we determine to be life-diminishing. The worst that could happen is that we are viewed as different, no fun, or a poor sport, which is not a huge price to pay for the life-gains we make by choosing to live by our own beliefs and values. We can share with people who have similar values, interests, and dreams for a more honest and sane, less violent world.

> Can I reject materialistic views that I feel are not healthy?
>
> My plan to live by my own values:

❖ Empowering ourselves by meeting our emotional needs

We have four basic emotional needs, usually not in our conscious awareness, which are:

1. *To belong.* To have this need met, we need meaningful relationships and interactions with spouses, partners, children, friends, and colleagues. Our behaviors need to be kind, honest, trustworthy, respectful, and appreciative so that people will want to be around us. Besides having significant relationships, we can participate in special interest groups, sports teams, spiritual organizations, or recovery groups to meet this emotional need that we have throughout our lifetime.

2. *To be someone.* This need involves feeling significant and competent. If this need is met, we realize our importance, not in a grandiose way, but as a created being who has a purpose in life that goes beyond the self. We acknowledge our strengths, are honest, live with integrity, and value ourselves. People are proud to be with us, and they speak highly of us.

3. *To be ourselves.* This need requires being who we really are, without facades. We are willing to share our thoughts, ideas, and feelings, we are emotionally balanced, and people experience us as *real.*

4. *To go beyond.* This emotional need is satisfied when we

continue to learn, have a spiritual connection, have moved beyond being preoccupied with self, and reach out to others in healthy and meaningful ways. Rather than stagnating, we continue to grow emotionally and move toward actualizing our potential.

As adults, part of our healing will be identifying our unfulfilled emotional needs and discovering healthy ways to satisfy these needs. When we are discontented and struggling with low self-esteem, we can decide what needs are not being met and discover ways to meet our emotional needs. Some of our needs are met by working on ourselves, and other emotional needs are met by connecting with other people and forming healthy relationships. When our basic needs are satisfied, our self-esteem is enhanced and we have a sense of well-being.

Emotional needs:
1. To belong
2. To be someone
3. To be ourselves
4. To go beyond

I can meet my emotional needs by:

❖ **Empowering ourselves if we are struggling with depression**

There are several reasons for depression, including:

- Past or present physical, sexual, or emotional abuse
- Dysfunction within our family of origin or current family
- Being controlled by another person or group
- Actively involved in an addiction
- Grieving personal losses
- Traumatic experiences brought on by war and other human tragedies
- Heredity
- Major transitions that are viewed as a loss
- Serious illness
- Side effects of medications
- Being overwhelmed because of being over-extended

Depression and hopelessness can also be due to actual or perceived *oppression*. We may be oppressed in a relationship, work system, or powerful group. When persons are oppressed and stripped of their rights, including making their own choices and being in charge of their life, it is very likely that they will experience depression.

To escape from our depressed feelings, we may try to self-medicate with alcohol, psych ourselves up, or stay away from our feelings by being constantly busy. However, these attempts at alleviating our depression are often futile. If we struggle with depression, there are many books, therapists, and clergy to help us with this difficult emotion. Don't hesitate to reach out for help.

My plan for depression:

❖ Empowering ourselves by recovering from co-dependency

When we are co-dependent, we merge with another person and expect them to make us happy and give us a reason for existing. We routinely sacrifice our time, resources, and even our core values in attempts to make relationships work. Our focus is on our partner, and we are concerned about what our partner is doing and not doing, saying or not saying, and the behaviors that are controlling, insensitive, confusing, and hurtful to us. We frequently allow our partners to invade our personal boundaries and steal our energy, freedom, and joy. We often let our mates make decisions for us and then blame them if the decisions turn out to be wrong. Co-dependency is also active when we think we are indispensable and act like martyrs in efforts to get attention and be loved. If we are male, we are often co-dependent on our work. If we are female, we are often co-dependent on our partners.

When we are co-dependent, we are so focused on the other person that we often fail to develop ourselves. We are co-dependent, not because we are unintelligent or inadequate, but because of how we were socialized and what we learned in our families of origin.

Typical thoughts and behaviors when we are co-dependent:

- ✓ I focus on *you* and submerge myself in you.
- ✓ I think you are more important than I am.
- ✓ I cannot live without you, and my life will end if you reject or leave me.
- ✓ My self-esteem is determined by your liking and approving of me.
- ✓ I try to solve your problems or relieve your pain, but direct little effort to do the same for myself.
- ✓ I am focused on pleasing you, at the expense of my own thoughts, beliefs, and values.

- ✓ I am not direct in asking you for what I need or stating my beliefs or limits.
- ✓ I need you to need me so that I feel better about myself.
- ✓ In our relationship, I sacrifice parts of myself by putting my own strengths, gifts, and interests aside. I spend my time sharing *your* interests and goals.
- ✓ I am unaware of what I feel, but I think I know how *you* feel.
- ✓ I am afraid that I will be abandoned if you are growing and thriving. If you have fewer needs, you will need me less.

Recovery from co-dependency starts with shifting the focus

Whenever we are dependent on a person or substance, our life experience is diminished. We cannot grow in self-esteem unless we eliminate, or at least modify, some or all of our dependent behaviors. Recovery from co-dependency starts with shifting the focus from people, activities, or substances to ourselves. By shifting the focus to ourselves, we are able to recognize our thoughts and behaviors that are creating problems for us.

Recovery from co-dependency involves taking responsibility for our lives and meeting many of our own emotional, physical, and spiritual needs. The reality is that we cannot be completed by another nor can we complete someone else. Our responsibility is to manage our own lives and discover happiness and wholeness within ourselves. We must first love, accept, and nurture ourselves before expecting others to love, accept, and nurture us. When we are able to do this, our relationships are inter-dependent rather than co-dependent.

- Nora shares her experience of feeling dependent:

    I always viewed myself as the dependent one in my marriage relationship. I tried to always be grateful that he chose such an inadequate person like me to be his wife. I didn't start the relationship believing this, but gradually, because of his negative remarks, this was my conclusion. I eventually realized that the only positive changes that I could make were within myself. This prompted me to detach from his negativity, return to college and create my own life. When I started moving forward, I felt a lot better and my self-esteem and self-confidence returned.

My co-dependency challenge:

❖ Empowering ourselves by thinking positively

We are the sole creators of our thoughts and our thoughts are powerful. Every thought or action that is hostile, critical, or demeaning of self or others will result in personal upheaval, illness, limitation, or losses at some point in our lives. There are few physical, emotional, or behavioral problems or illnesses that are not created or healed, to some degree, by the mind (Hay 1999). Spiritual teachers emphasize that there are no external causes involved in what we are experiencing in life. Since we create our reality with our thoughts, the responsibility for our life experiences is placed directly upon each one of us. How we think is what we will attract into our lives and what we will become. We generate misery or happiness, depending on our thoughts, attitudes, beliefs, and behaviors. Thinking positively enhances our psychological, emotional, spiritual, and physical health. Our immune system is strengthened. When our thoughts are positive, we place ourselves in higher energy levels, where there is less emotional and physical turmoil.

We can dwell in the highest levels of energy and consciousness by feeding our minds *healthy mind food*, or we can let our minds roam around in negativity, which ushers in low levels of energy. It is like using our computers. An unlimited amount of information can be accessed that is healthy and expands our minds. In contrast, there are websites that have negative and disgusting information and photos. As we grow in self-esteem, we become keenly aware of the importance of staying away from negative mind food, which is anything we see, do, or hear that is violent, evil, and life-diminishing. If we are thinking, speaking, and living negatively, we are putting ourselves in energy levels where there is more emotional, spiritual, and physical illness. The choice is ours. We can think in ways that shoot ourselves in the foot or, through positive thinking, create experiences that are life-enhancing.

When our thoughts are positive, we experience enhanced health on all levels of our being. If we think that life is interesting, life will be interesting. If we think that life is supported by a loving God, those thoughts will manifest and we will experience peace, beauty, and love in our daily lives.

I need to think more positively, especially when…

The benefits to myself by thinking more positively will be:

> **Since we create our reality with our thoughts, the responsibility for our life experience is placed directly upon each one of us.**

Chapter 8

Reflecting, Processing, and Discovering Ourselves

Life was meant to be lived, and curiosity must be kept alive. We must never, for whatever reason, turn our back on life.
—Eleanor Roosevelt

In the early stages of our low self-esteem recovery, the thought of loving, respecting, valuing, appreciating, and embracing ourselves may have seemed very strange, uncomfortable, vain, and selfish. As we recover from low self-esteem, we are increasingly able to respect, love, value, appreciate, and celebrate ourselves.

This chapter has several activities that help us to self-reflect, process our thoughts and feelings, and learn more about ourselves. We can be assured that we will discover inner strength and special qualities about ourselves as we continue on our recovery and empowerment journey.

Project 1:

- **Create a lifeline**

To gain more awareness about yourself, reflect on your

childhood and other significant experiences up to the present time. Draw a line that has high points and low points indicating the major life experiences that significantly impacted you. Do this in a way that is most meaningful to you. Use photographs, drawings, or other creative ways to highlight the significant experiences in your life. Start with your first childhood recollection. From that memory, plot your positive and negative experiences. Caution: some persons experienced deep emotional trauma in their childhoods and to survive, have suppressed the painful memories and feelings. If this is your experience and you find this exercise to be frightening or emotionally painful, seek professional help and start an emotional healing process.

Once you have completed your lifeline, write in your journal about the high points and low points that you have indicated. You may want to use the following questions:

Question 1: When did I discover (if I did) that I was inadequate, incapable, or unlovable?

Look at the low points in your lifeline. The purpose of this question is to raise your awareness as to when you started to think that you were not okay, if that is what happened. You have always been involved with other people, and from your interactions with them, you were constantly learning and drawing conclusions about yourself. As children, we accepted what we heard from adults and were not able to reject false or distorted information. If your experiences with significant others were esteem-diminishing, you are likely to be viewing your present life experience through your negative thoughts and beliefs about yourself. As adults, we can identify what we learned and realize that if we believe that we are inadequate, incapable, and unlovable, we need to discard this false information.

Question 2: Who were the significant and most influential persons in my life?

Look at the lower points in your lifeline. As an infant, you had healthy self-esteem. However, as you moved out of infancy to being a young child and then an adolescent, you may have had interactions with adults that caused you to lose your natural, innocent love of self. Recall some of the negative communications that were directed to you, and journal about how your self-esteem was affected.

Now, spend some time with the high points on your lifeline. Identify and write down the persons who spent time with you and provided love and encouragement. Think about the positive qualities they shared with you. Send your appreciation to them through your thoughts. You may also want to talk to them directly or write a letter on how much you appreciate them for being so supportive to you in your childhood.

Question 3: What do you know about the childhood history and the emotional issues of the significant adults or peers who influenced your self-esteem?

Return to the low points on your lifeline. This question is not suggesting that you blame parents or other caretakers. Rather, it helps you to identify the true source of the harmful actions or words, rather than blaming yourself. Many parents model the ways they were parented. Parents who were emotionally, verbally, sexually, or physically abused or punished in punitive ways when they were children are at a higher risk for doing the same to their own children.

If you struggle with low self-esteem, you may never know why your parents, caretakers, or other adults did not treat you with respect and attend to your emotional needs. They might refuse to listen to your memories and your perspective. They may act like they are listening, but do not take you seriously. They are likely to deny any wrongdoing. If this is true, don't give up. Continue your healing process and work through your emotional pain by journaling or optimally, working with a therapist or support group.

Now look at the high points in your lifeline. Spend some time thinking about the persons who were supportive and fostered your self-esteem. What were their personal qualities, and what do you remember about your interactions with them?

Question 4: What did I learn about myself in my childhood that I still believe as an adult?

Take some time to view your lifeline and experience your uniqueness. This is your life, and these are your memories. Some of your experiences were painful; some were learning experiences; and some were high points in your life. You may want to write about your overall life experience, as indicated on your lifeline.

Project 2:

- **Raise your awareness by journaling**

Writing in a journal is a way to discover more about yourself. Here are some sentences that may help you get started:

Reflecting, Processing, and Discovering Ourselves

- The last time I cried, it was about…

- What has been my greatest accomplishment?

- Describe your day and indicate the amount of stress you experienced:

- What my partner/friends say when I make a bad choice is:

- What I remember my father saying when I made a bad choice was:

- When I am upset and want comfort, I go to:

- The person who encourages me the most is…

- The kind of person I would like to be is…

- I am the happiest when…

Project 3:

- **Acknowledge your strengths**

To recover from feeling inferior, it is helpful to write down what we learned about ourselves. On the chart below, write down your weaknesses, based on what you were told. Then write down your strengths.

My weaknesses:	My strengths:
Example: I was told that I am stubborn and dumb and still believe it.	Example: I stand up for what I believe, and I learn easily if it is something of interest to me.

Look at all of your strengths and imagine how they can be used to your benefit and the benefit of others.

Project 4:

- **Be proud of your emotional achievements**

Our internal emotional achievements are just as important as the achievements that are seen by other people. As this quote says: *The best day of your life is the one on which you decide your life is your own. No apologies or excuses. No one to lean on, rely on, or blame. The gift is yours—it is an amazing journey—and you alone are responsible for the quality of it. This is the day your life really begins.*—Bob Moawad

Our emotional achievements may involve becoming more honest with ourselves and others, being able to self-advocate, being more self-confident, and being more direct with people, including telling them how important they are to us.

We know we have made emotional gains when we can make

statements such as:

> I take full responsibility for my life.
> My self-talk is positive.
> I am emotionally honest with myself and others.
> I am acknowledging and appreciating my feelings.
> I feel emotionally centered and balanced.
> I like nurturing myself.
> I am discovering and appreciating my gifts, talents, and interests.
> I fully accept and embrace myself.
> I appreciate who I am.

My emotional achievements:

My emotional achievements have improved my life in the following ways:

Project 5:

- **Acknowledge and work with your anger**

There are many reasons for having legitimate anger, especially when we experience mental, emotional, physical, verbal and spiritual abuse. Along with our right to be angry comes a responsibility to express our anger in healthy ways that do not harm ourselves or others. The following are healthy and appropriate ways to work with anger:

- **Journal about your anger**

Use the following partial sentences to get started:

- The real reason I am angry is:
- The person I am angry at is…
- I am angry at what happened in my childhood:
- What I learned about anger from my father was…
- When my mother was angry, she…

When we journal our angry feelings, we begin to understand our anger more clearly. When we are ready, we can release the angry feelings.

- **Use self-calming strategies**

Breathing deeply is the best way to relax your body. When you feel anger rising within you, breathing deeply will help you remain calm and in control of your anger. Taking the time to breathe will also give you a few moments to decide how you are going to respond to a situation that is creating anger. When breathing, visualize your anger leaving your body, both the anger you know about and the anger you are possibly carrying that is not in your awareness. As you breathe, imagine the anger leaving and being replaced by positive energy flowing into your mind and body.

- **Speak directly to the person**

Rather than suppressing our anger and resentments, we need to express our feelings assertively in attempts to create change in a relationship. This should only be done if there is guaranteed physical safety. In schools, the potential victims of bullies are trained to self-advocate and say, "Please stop bullying me!" We can do the same in our adult relationships and insist that abusive or inappropriate behaviors or statements stop. With people who have a strong need to control, the behaviors may continue. However, we are self-advocating, which is esteem-enhancing, rather than accepting a powerless victim role, which is esteem-diminishing.

- **Exercise in non-competitive ways to release anger**

Body movement is helpful to release angry feelings. Taking a brisk walk, jogging, or hitting balls in a racquetball court, punching a punching bag, lifting weights, twisting a towel, or hitting pillows are good ways to release anger. Some people use a small, flat drum and drum out percussion patterns to release their anger. Besides being an outlet for the anger, physical activity produces endorphins that will help you feel better. If the exercise is routine and you don't have to actively engage your mind, you can visualize the anger being released from your body as you exercise.

- **Do anger work outdoors in nature**

Processing and releasing your anger can be done while doing outdoor activities such as cleaning up branches, planting trees, raking, doing landscape work, chopping wood, or planting and weeding a garden. Anger can also be released by throwing stones into a body of water, and hiking or biking on the nature trails.

- **Express your anger through movement**

When you harbor anger, your physical body is involved as well as your mind. You may be able to release your anger by using your mind, but combining thoughts with body movement is even more effective. Allow yourself to feel your feelings. Verbalize your anger and use your body to express and possibly exaggerate your emotions, including your anger. You may want to create and act out a serious or a humorous performance to release your anger and stress. Holler and scream if it feels helpful and if you have privacy.

- **Talk out your anger with a person you trust**

Talking with a trusted friend who understands how important it is to express feelings, including anger, can be very helpful. However, you don't want to overload your friends by having the same conversation repeatedly. There are interactions that relieve stress and others that create higher levels of stress. You may decide to seek out an anger class or support group if your anger is intense, pervasive, and routinely creating problems for you and your relationships.

- **Be productive with your anger**

Invest the anger energy into doing various jobs such as yard work, cleaning, shoveling snow, washing a vehicle, or other physical tasks. These activities can also provide some relief from the intense anger feelings and give you a time-out to sort through your feelings, gain perspective, and make healthy choices about what you need to do.

- **Join a support group, such as a Twelve-Step Program**

Twelve-Step recovery groups change people's lives, not only because the members have sobriety, but the program offers a spiritual way to live, an emotionally safe place to express feelings, and a sponsor to support you as you work the Program. In Twelve-Step groups, people express their anger and other feelings appropriately, and with honesty. Participating in these groups may be your first experience with people sharing their feelings so openly. Recovery and other types of support groups are safe places to express your anger or other feelings because you will not be judged, criticized, or shamed. Healing happens in support groups, as evidenced by members' positive changes in behaviors, which result in healthier relationships and a sense of emotional well-being.

- **Process your anger with music**

Listening to, playing, or creating music that is bold and powerful will help you get in touch with your anger. Sing along with music that has lyrics that help you to identify and describe your experiences and feelings. Some parts of classical music that bring up images of anger, marching music, or some of the current popular music that elicits emotions can be helpful to express and release your anger in effective and non-harmful ways.

- **Attend a retreat, workshop, or healing session**

There are anger retreats or group therapy opportunities where you can join with others in expressing and releasing your anger. If you travel to a different town and are with people you have never met and will never see again, you will have fewer inhibitions. When you see others working through their anger, you will be more able to give yourself permission to experience and express your anger. You will hear people sharing stories that resonate with your own life experiences. As with any anger work, you have to put aside self-directives such as, "be nice, don't share feelings, always speak with kind words, and don't ever express your anger." We can release anger in ways that are not harmful to ourselves or others.

- **Visualize the person who has been abusive to you and talk to her/him**

Face an empty chair and create an image in your mind of the person who harmed you or who is currently harming you. Stand up to feel more powerful as you speak to the imaginary person in the chair. Do not censor your words. Say everything you need to say in any way that helps you to release your anger. Let all of your feelings out without minimizing the hurt you experienced. This is also an effective way to rehearse what you will say if you choose to actually meet and confront the person who harmed you.

- **Transform your anger energy into positive creations or actions**

Transform the anger energy by drawing, creating music, or doing crafts or other hobbies. Invest your anger energy in activities that you consider to be healthy and worthwhile, such as becoming a child advocate, a Red Cross volunteer, or joining others to support veterans or work for the elimination of child abuse.

- **Use the Serenity Prayer**

You can reduce a considerable amount of your anger by daily embracing the wisdom of the Serenity Prayer: *God grant me the serenity to accept the things I cannot change, courage to change the things I can, and wisdom to know the difference.*

- **Use mental imagery and visualize your anger leaving your body**

You can use your creative mind to form mental pictures. There may be anger that you are aware of and anger that is below your level of awareness. Visualize all of the anger as being released from your mind, emotions, and physical body. Besides anger, you can visualize other negativity leaving you. At the end of a visualization session, imagine a place that is peaceful and calming, breathe deeply, and return slowly into full awareness.

I am angry because:	My plan to work with my anger:

Project 6:

- **Reflect on your relationships**

Journal about what is positive and what is negative in your primary relationship. Here are some questions that may be helpful:

- ✓ What was the level of your self-esteem when you entered your primary relationship, and what is the *current* level of your self-esteem? Journal about any changes in your self-esteem.
- ✓ Do you feel that your partner and you create an equal *team* where there is cooperation and sharing of family responsibilities?
- ✓ Do you feel controlled in your current relationship?
- ✓ Are you being criticized too often for no valid reason?

✓ Does your partner always have to be the center of attention?
✓ Is your partner overly dependent on you?
✓ Am I staying in a dysfunctional relationship because I believe I don't deserve any better?

It is not uncommon to be unaware of what is involved in a healthy relationship because our family of origin was dysfunctional. The following are descriptors of a **healthy relationship**:

➢ There is physical and emotional safety in the relationship
➢ There is equal personal power, rather than one person controlling the other
➢ Participants are honest and open with their feelings in an appropriate way
➢ Participants listen attentively to each other
➢ Judging statements are not made, such as, "Are you done now?" (spoken sarcastically) or, "You're too sensitive," or, "You shouldn't feel that way!"
➢ Participants in the relationship feel respected and valued
➢ People take ownership of their part of the problem when conflicts arise
➢ Rather than blaming one another, partners negotiate fairly and compromise
➢ Both persons feel that they are significant to the other person and there is healthy closeness rather than possessiveness
➢ There is mutual caring and nurturing in both words and actions
➢ Both persons move beyond their own individual egos and extend caring to the other
➢ Both people are encouraging, cooperative, interesting, and communicative
➢ Partners *invest* time in the relationship

> Healthy partners frequently communicate affirming statements such as, "You are important and significant in my life," and "I appreciate and love you!" Behaviors are congruent with these statements.

Strengths in my primary relationship:	Weaknesses in my primary relationship:
Our improvement plan:	

Project 7:

- **Make amends and forgive yourself**

We need to make amends if we have caused harm to another person. The next step is to forgive ourselves rather than berating ourselves for long periods of time. Learning from mistakes, accepting them as opportunities for growth, and moving on are part of a journey that we may take several times in a lifetime.

> I need to make amends to:
>
> I need to forgive myself for:

Project 8:

- **Write about what you like about yourself**

Stop and think about the qualities you really like about yourself. This may be a new experience! If you need some help, ask your trusted friends what they like about you. You may want to do this over many days, because other things will come up as you are driving, showering, waiting in line, or whenever you are thinking about this project.

> The qualities I like about myself:

Project 9:

- **Relish compliments that you receive**

When we have low self-esteem and believe we are inferior and inadequate, we fail to hear and relish compliments because they are in conflict with what we believe about ourselves. To help ourselves

Reflecting, Processing, and Discovering Ourselves

grow in self-esteem, we need to listen attentively to compliments and be grateful to whoever is affirming us. By doing this, we honor what the other person is saying. If the compliment is contrary to a negative belief we have about ourselves, rather than discounting or ignoring the compliment, we can accept what is said and change our belief to be more accurate and positive.

Rather than reading greeting cards quickly and putting them aside, you may want to save them and re-read them several times, especially on difficult days. This will help to renew your energies and uplift your spirit. By doing this, you will see more of what your friends see as your strengths that may be hidden from your awareness, or that you haven't acknowledged, because you were taught to be modest.

Write down the compliments people have given you regarding your work or your positive personality traits. Review your list often. Make this an ongoing project.

The compliment:	My response:

Project 10:

- **Reflect on your miraculous body and mind**

Sometimes we are very disrespectful of our body, by the food we eat or by not exercising. We complain if we have pain, but often

◄ Self-Esteem

ignore our bodies when we are experiencing good health. Seldom do we take the time to truly appreciate our miraculous body and mind.

Appreciate Your Amazing Body
(Author unknown)

1. Feel your pulse. Your heart beats about 100 thousand times a day, circulating blood through your body. Your body contains eight pints of blood. Within a tiny droplet of blood, there are some five million red blood cells, 300 thousand platelets, and 10 thousand white cells. About 400 gallons of blood flow through your kidneys in one day. Placed end to end, all your body's blood vessels would measure about 62 thousand miles.
2. Notice your breath. You breathe about 20 times per minute, more than 10 million times per year. The surface area of the lungs is roughly the same size as a tennis court. Your left lung is smaller than your right lung to make room for your heart. You lose two cups of water a day through breathing.
3. Feel your skin. Each square inch of your skin contains four yards of nerve fibers, 100 sweat glands, three million cells, and three yards of blood vessels.
4. Blink your eyes. You blink your eyes about 20 thousand times a day. An eyelash lives about 150 days before it falls out. Each of your eyes has 120 million rods, which helps you see in black and white. Each eye has six million cones, which help you see in color.
5. Smile. You use about 17 facial muscles for a smile and about 43 for a frown.
6. Think. There are 100 billion neurons in our brain. We have between 30,000 and 50,000 thoughts each day. We have little knowledge of how our brain works, the mental potential

Reflecting, Processing, and Discovering Ourselves

that we have, and how the brain can be connected to all of the other parts of our body.
7. Our cells communicate with each other and each cell has equal importance. Our cells are creative and can think thoughts that we have never thought before.
8. We have more than 250 types of cells that all work together to sustain our lives. If we would design our lives like what happens within our healthy bodies at a cellular level, we would have harmony, cooperation, giving, receiving kindness and love within ourselves.

Our physical bodies are awesome. Realizing the amazing aspects of our body and mind helps us to truly respect and value ourselves. Rather than ignoring our body and complaining when a part of our body is sending out pain signals, we can love and appreciate our body and mind each and every day.

Journal about your appreciation of your body and mind:

Project 11:

- **Act out emotions with body movement**

You can do this exercise with or without music. Relax and feel your emotions as your body expresses these experiences:

➤ Being strong and, in contrast, being gentle
➤ Going inward and reaching outward

Self-Esteem

- Experiencing victory and experiencing defeat
- Being open to life or closed to life
- Carving out personal space, keeping others out of your personal space, and inviting people to come into your personal space
- Being happy or sad
- Sharing your feelings and suppressing feelings
- Being grateful
- Experiencing serenity and peacefulness

You may also want to express yourself in body movement and sing along about *your own self* in love songs such as *Because You Loved Me* by Celine Dion, *Lean on Me* by Al Green, *I Will Always Love You,* by Whitney Houston or Dolly Parton, *Everything I Do,* by Brian Adams, *Love Song* by Adele, or *I Hope You Dance* by Lee Ann Womack.

When I do these body movements, I experience:

Project 12:

- **Describe yourself**

For the purpose of this project, try limiting yourself to four words. In this way, you will be describing your most important attributes.

1	
2.	
3.	
4.	

Project 13:

- **Feel emotionally powerful, capable, and resilient**

There will be times when we are treated unfairly and we feel powerless, but we don't want to victimize ourselves by *expecting* to be treated unfairly. Nor do we want to feel powerless when we actually have a fair amount of personal power. Our powerless feelings and victim mentality will fade away when we invest time and energy into learning effective ways to communicate and other life-skills; and continually up-grading our occupational skills. Being life-long learners results in being and feeling capable, which is an emotion that fuels healthy self-esteem. Resiliency is a by-product of self-esteem and helps us to weather the storms and losses in life.

I feel powerless when:	I feel powerful when:
I can reduce my powerless feelings by:	I feel capable when:
	I need to be resilient when:

Project 14:

- **Set goals for yourself**

Think about what you want to achieve in life and set goals.

- My emotional life:

- My mental life:

- My physical body:

- My spirituality:

- My relationships:

- My work:

Be confident in your ability to meet your goals. A good reminder is: *Whoever you are, there is some younger person who thinks you are perfect. There is some work that will never be done if you don't do it. There is someone who would miss you if you were gone. There is a place that you alone can fill.* Jacob M. Braude

Project 15:
- **Use your mind to visualize**

Visualize and form mental pictures regarding:

- ✓ Each cell in your body having perfect intelligence, working together with your other cells to create perfect health

- ✓ Living without toxic guilt and feeling free
- ✓ Achieving a goal that you want to achieve
- ✓ Changing a dysfunctional behavior that is creating havoc and emotional pain in your life
- ✓ Feeling confident when interacting with people, and enjoying the conversations
- ✓ Speaking, teaching a class, or playing a musical instrument even better than you are currently performing
- ✓ Saying, "I can!"

> Describe your visualization:

Project 16:

- **Look within for happiness**

We are socialized into believing that finding the right person and having the luxuries of life will make us happy and content. Though healthy relationships certainly contribute to our happiness, lasting happiness springs from an internal source. Happiness is more likely to be experienced if we develop a relationship with ourselves that is nurturing, creative, stimulating, and peaceful. We can discover what energizes us and gives us purpose and design our lives accordingly. Being happy requires thinking about what we *do* have, rather than what we don't have. We can be grateful that we are thinking about happiness, when so many people are struggling to stay safe, fed and clothed. And life teaches us that we can't keep happiness unless we are willing to pass on the positive energies of happiness to the people that we meet in life.

Journal about times you have felt happy and contented:

Journal about your plans for your own happiness:

Project 17:

- **Think about joyful experiences**

Reflecting on joyful experiences is a way to celebrate ourselves and our life.

I feel joyful when I am alone and doing…

I feel joyful when I am with others, especially…

I can create joy for myself by…

Project 18:

- **Write your own personal affirmations**

Affirmations are positive, active statements, affirming what is happening in the present moment. Examples:

- My life keeps getting better and better.
- I am excited about life, and I am glad to be alive.
- I am grateful that I can create and design my life the way I want it.
- I love my miraculous mind!
- Positive energy flows freely through me.
- I let myself feel all of my emotions.
- I laugh easily and share my laughter with others.
- I am healing in all areas of mind, body, and spirit.

Keep your list of affirmations on your refrigerator, in your planner, or wherever it is noticeable and convenient to review. Refer to your list often. Expand your list.

My affirmations:

Project 19:

- **Practice *present moment meditations* of gratitude**

At any moment, stop your thoughts and breathe deeply to relax. Focus on the present moment. Think about what blessings you have received in order to experience this particular moment. For example, you are working, or you are attending a concert. What had to happen in your life to be able to do these activities? You can reflect on your blessings, such as:

- I am blessed with a good mind and body so that I can work.
- I am mobile so I can be at work or attend a concert.
- I am blessed with good hearing and vision.
- I have transportation to get to the places I need or want to go.
- I have an income so I am able to pay my bills, as well as pay for the activities that I love.
- My blessings include being able to afford clothing appropriate for the weather or event.

Wherever you are—waiting for a train, waiting for children to finish with their lessons, while getting a haircut, before going to sleep—your present moment meditations will center you, direct you to focus on the positives in your life, and remind you of how many blessings you are receiving. Increasingly, you will live in gratefulness!

My *present moment meditation*:

Project 20:

- **Create a list of reasons to be grateful**

Examples:

- I am grateful for my family.
- I am grateful for having meaningful work, good health, and an intelligent mind.
- I am grateful for my sight, hearing, and mobility.
- I am grateful for having supportive and trustworthy friends.
- I am grateful for having a high quality of life.

My reasons to be grateful:

Project 21:

- **Discover healthy ways to share yourself**

We are able to love others in healthy ways when we have learned to love ourselves. When we are in touch with our emotional and spiritual selves, we readily share ourselves by expressing our feelings, ideas, dreams, ideals, values, stories, and plans. Emotionally closed people too often take their loving feelings to their grave, never having expressed them to those they loved in their lifetime, assuming

◄ Self-Esteem

that they knew. We can't take for granted that people know we care about them. We have voices, language, and many other ways to communicate our love. For the people we love, there never should be a doubt that we love them.

Loving well and sharing ourselves also involves being good stewards of the blessings we have been given. Sharing our resources can be done with time, energy, money, knowledge, and personal strengths and talents. We discover that there is no end to the places that welcome our healthy energy and resources.

We all have something to give to our world. We share ourselves when we share our emotions: love, kindness, joy, understanding, sympathy, acceptance, and forgiveness. We share ourselves when we share our spirituality: prayer, vision, beauty, peace, and faith. We share ourselves when we give from our heart: caring, support, encouragement, and inspiration. We share ourselves when we listen: to a child, to a significant other, to a friend, or to a person who may experience emotional healing because of being heard. Kindness, empathy, compassion, and gentleness are of key importance to give to ourselves and to others on a daily basis. Loving well and sharing ourselves are not just nice things to do. Loving well and sharing ourselves add meaning to our lives.

My ways of sharing myself:

Chapter 9

Respecting and Valuing Ourselves

> *'Each of us is in truth an idea of the Great Gull, an unlimited idea of freedom,'* Jonathan would say in the evenings on the beach, *'And precision flying is a step toward expressing our real nature. Everything that limits us we have to put aside.'* —Bach

Our self-esteem recovery journey has involved respecting and valuing ourselves. Our lives have changed dramatically for the better. We are more confident in our ability to think rationally, be assertive, protect our boundaries, and make life-fostering decisions. Our understanding of ourselves has grown, and we feel good about being who we are, what we are doing, and how we are doing it. Knowing that we are capable and competent has given us a sense of control over our lives. We esteem and celebrate ourselves. We feel like we have *come home* to our real self.

Respecting, valuing, and appreciating ourselves comes from a quiet inner knowing that we are honoring life by being our best self. Our behaviors are in alignment with our values, and we live our lives with integrity. We no longer search for people's validation or approval because we are able to validate and approve of ourselves.

We are seldom lonely because we enjoy our own company and interests. Rather than being harsh with ourselves, we are supportive to ourselves in challenging times. We realize that we have an awesome mind and body; and also a strong spirit. Knowing that our growth journey has no end point, we are motivated to continue to learn and grow in wisdom.

We are all creative persons and have many ways to respect and value ourselves. The following are some ways to continue on our life journey in the spirit of respecting, valuing, embracing, and appreciating ourselves:

❖ **We respect, value, embrace, and appreciate ourselves by:**

Trusting and living our inner truth

Most of us have to learn to listen and trust our inner truth. Our inner truth is our spirit-truth, our intuitive sense working within us. We are socialized to follow external directives, so most of us base our beliefs, values, and actions on parental and cultural directives. As we experience more awareness, recovery, and personal growth, we increasingly pattern our life around our own life-fostering values and beliefs. When we live from our inner truth, we are living from the center of our being and are guided in the journey of reaching our potential. We come to realize that we are *spiritual* beings living in a physical body and that every person is created for an important purpose, including ourselves.

Respecting and Valuing Ourselves

> Reflecting on my inner truth:

❖ **We respect, value, embrace, and appreciate ourselves by:**

Mentally, physically, emotionally and spiritually nurturing ourselves

Self-care is never being selfish. It is our responsibility to take care of our gift of life. Nurturing ourselves on the mental dimension involves staying mentally active and having positive thoughts and self-talk. Self-nurturing on the physical dimension requires healthy nutrition, exercise, minimizing stress, and sleeping regularly. Accepting our feelings, including the more difficult feeling of anger, and expressing our emotions appropriately or writing in a journal are ways to nurture ourselves on the emotional level. Spiritual nurturing involves praying, contemplating, meditating, recognizing the miracle and sacredness of life, and living with spiritual principles such as valuing, respecting, loving, appreciating, and honoring ourselves and all others.

Self-Esteem

> My plan for mentally self-nurturing:
>
> My plan for physically self-nurturing:
>
> My plan for emotionally self-nurturing:
>
> My plan for spiritually self-nurturing:

- ❖ **We respect, value, embrace, and appreciate ourselves by:**

    Acknowledging our giftedness

    We are all gifted, although we may not have flashy gifts that will make us a super-star or millionaire. However, some of the most humble gifts are the most powerful because they often change people's lives for the better. We may be gifted and very skilled in the following areas that positively affect people's lives:

    - Listening
    - Encouraging
    - Teaching
    - Empowering others by helping them to develop their skills and talents
    - Modeling kindness, honesty, and living with integrity
    - Accepting others as they are
    - Sharing resources, including time

- Touching or hugging in ways that clearly communicate, "I care about you."
- Believing in someone
- Being patient
- Sharing feelings
- Being creative
- Being able to envision something better, more beautiful, or something more meaningful
- Having wisdom

As we grow in self-esteem, we will increasingly embrace our skills, talents, and uniqueness, and discover meaningful ways to use them in ways that benefit ourselves and others.

My gifts and strengths:

I can use my gifts and strengths by:

❖ **We respect, value, embrace, and appreciate ourselves by:**

Identifying our goals and activating

We have a responsibility to orchestrate and launch our life, rather than stay in *park* and stagnate. We can be successful in accomplishing what we want to accomplish if we believe in ourselves, are self-confident, have health and authentic self-esteem, and trust God's guidance and help. We will connect with the right persons on our journey, which will affirm that we are on the right path. We will know where we belong, what we are meant to do, and feel that our life is purposeful.

My life design:

My plan to achieve my goals:

❖ **We respect, value, embrace, and appreciate ourselves by:**

Living one day at a time

Personal goals become our reality when we concentrate on living one day at a time and doing what we need to do, each day. Rather than thinking about the past or worrying about the future, we realize that our energies only make a difference in the present. We can cherish each present moment and be continually grateful for family, friends and our many other blessings.

Letting go of the past would require me to:

Letting go of worrying about the future would require me to:

Living just for today would help me to:

❖ **We respect, value, embrace, and appreciate ourselves by:**

Becoming energy-efficient

We have a certain amount of energy, and most of us are in charge of how we use our energy, unlike many people around the world who have no choice but to use their energies to survive. Although we may have the freedom to choose how to use our energy, we may be wasting our energy in various ways. When we engage in negative self-talk, worrying, are fearful and overly-critical, our energy is being used, but we have nothing to show for it except negative feelings. We may be a perfectionist, wasting energy on trivial details. We may be a compulsive shopper, frantically buying and then returning the items we bought on the following day. There may be people in our lives who are energy-takers. When we are with them, we feel exhausted and drained of our energy.

Becoming energy-efficient is using our energy in ways that make a difference. Efficient and effective use of energy often involves *making things better*. There is no limit to where we can make things better—teaching, mentoring, creating, repairing, remodeling, cleaning, cooking, organizing, listening, designing, supporting, challenging, volunteering, and many other activities that are involved in *making things better*. This is using our personal energy efficiently, effectively, and purposefully.

> My personal energy is wasted when I:
>
> I am efficient and effective with my energy when I:
>
> Being energy-efficient creates the feeling of:
>
> My plan to become more energy-efficient:

❖ **We respect, value, embrace, and appreciate ourselves by:**

Thinking and living creatively

Thinking and living creatively involves exploring new ideas, checking out different viewpoints, generating alternatives, and choosing the best option or plan. As we grow in clarity of thought, we can better discern the true from the false. We become more adept at stepping up to the decision line to make necessary and difficult choices because we realize that *not* making a choice is *making* a choice.

When we experience losses, such as a relationship or job, retirement, financial stress, or other difficulties in life, we are challenged to creatively redesign our lives. Likewise, if we are struggling with a debilitating illness and lose physical capabilities, thinking creatively is necessary so that we utilize all of our abilities, despite our disabilities.

Thinking and living creatively involves taking risks, not always knowing where our choices will lead us, what will be involved, or if there will be a good outcome. It is learning what works and what doesn't work in our life. Thinking and living creatively is putting ourselves on the line of challenge to test ourselves repeatedly to see different aspects of ourselves, to revisit what we know about ourselves, and to explore what we don't know. It is stretching and expanding ourselves. If we think and live creatively, we truly give life our best efforts.

> Reflecting on thinking and living creatively:

❖ **We respect, value, embrace, and appreciate ourselves by:**

Standing up for what we believe

Rather than avoiding the emotional unpleasantness of being controversial, our healthy self-esteem will help us advocate for healthy changes, even though it would be easier to remain silent. We need to say "no" to what is unfair, unjust, and oppressive and respond with a hearty "yes" to healthy challenges that feel right for us.

> My basic beliefs:
>
>
> A situation where I need to stand up for my beliefs:

◀ Self-Esteem

❖ **We respect, value, embrace, and appreciate ourselves by:**

Being in harmony with universal laws

Thoughts, words, and actions that we send out will, at some point in time, return to us. If we affirm and treat others with kindness, love, and encouragement, we will be treated in the same way. When we are mean-spirited and abusive to others, we will experience the same treatment. If we have the right motivations when we reach out to others and are giving without expectations of receiving in return, we can trust the universal law to provide abundance in our lives.

Universal Law of Love: Love is our true nature and the most powerful energy for healing and transforming ourselves and serving others. We can share our love with everyone we meet by offering a smile, word, compliment, prayer, understanding, or encouragement. When we give healthy love to others and feel loved, we thrive on all dimensions of our being.

Universal Law of Gratitude: The more grateful our hearts, the more we experience the goodness and abundance that God provides for us. *God loves gratitude.* Love and gratitude are the highest forms of energy and foster health and well-being. People who live in gratitude are grateful for all of the people, places, and experiences that make life so interesting and emotionally rewarding to live.

Reflecting on the universal laws:

My plan for living in harmony with universal laws:

❖ **We respect, value, embrace, and appreciate ourselves by:**

*Connecting with people and activities
that are positive and stimulating*

Primary relationships and friendships that are mutually positive and stimulating keep us in the realm of high energy. Making new discoveries about ourselves, other people, and the world creates excitement and enthusiasm for life. By sharing time with people who are positive and interesting, and participating in meaningful activities, we stay active on our mental, emotional, physical, and spiritual levels of being.

We can reflect on what interests us and become skilled at a hobby or invest our time and energy into an area entirely different than we have ever done. We may return to an old interest that was left behind because we became busy doing other things. Challenging activities that require learning will keep our minds active. Continuing to learn in our occupation and continuing to improve a skill or talent are life-enhancing. There are mental and emotional benefits to being lifelong learners.

Stimulating people:

Stimulating activities:

I would like to spend more time doing:

❖ **We respect, value, embrace, and appreciate ourselves by:**

Laughing often

Research confirms repeatedly that laughter has a healing effect on the body, so it is important to lighten up, hang loose, chill out, and see the humor in many of our experiences. Why does laughing make us feel better? Laughter releases chemicals called endorphins, which are the body's natural painkillers. Humor and laughter strengthen our immune system, help us recover from illness, and elevate our sense of well-being. When we have humor in our lives, we are less likely to struggle with negative emotions. Laughing relaxes the body and reduces problems associated with high blood pressure, strokes, arthritis, and ulcers. Not only is laughter an excellent way to lift our mood, it is *internal* exercise for the body. There is not a system in the body that a hearty laugh doesn't stimulate. Gravitating toward people who are humorous and help us to laugh is important for our health. We can visualize our energies and all of our cells rejoicing as we burst out in hearty laughter. Life is too serious to be too serious!

What I experience as humorous:

❖ **We respect, value, embrace, and appreciate ourselves by:**

Treating ourselves like our own best friend

We are very willing to take time and support good friends when their life is falling apart or stressful. We accept and love our special friends, rather than being critical or judgmental. Our friendships are healing, comforting, and nurturing. We can have the same kind of supportive relationship with ourselves, and love, accept, respect, be empathic, and treat ourselves with kindness. We can celebrate and savor our successes, saying to ourselves, "Good job!" Or, "It's absolutely amazing that I did that!"

> I can be my own best friend by:

❖ **We respect, value, embrace, and appreciate ourselves by:**

Being open to the many forms of healing

Alternative, noninvasive, natural techniques are increasingly being used for preventing illness, maintaining health, and helping us to heal when we are ill. Relaxation techniques, the many forms of meditation, deep-breathing and energy techniques, different forms of massage, Tai Chi, Qigong, and yoga are all forms of healing and nurturing our mental, emotional, physical, and spiritual self. Naturopathy is a preventative technique that involves massage, nutrition, heat, water, and exercise. Most of these forms of healing are not aligned with any religion or sect, contrary to what many people believe.

Meditation is growing in popularity due to its numerous health benefits. To meditate is to turn inward, to concentrate on the inner self. Meditative techniques are effective in transforming negative thinking into positive thinking, and changing agitated feelings to a more peaceful emotional state. Other benefits are deep levels of relaxation, decreased muscle tension, increased serotonin levels, and pain reduction. Meditating on a certain part of the body increases the blood flow to that area, and the cells receive more oxygen. Some meditation techniques are concentrative, involving focusing, and other techniques allow for the free flow of thoughts. Meditation is an experience that often results in a feeling of emotional balance and inner peace.

Body movement techniques, such as Tai Chi and Qigong, result in a clear and calmer mind, deep and restorative relaxation, and increased energy that more freely moves within the body. Metabolism and digestion often become more efficient. These techniques usher in a higher level of intuition, creativity, and spiritual experiences, including synchronous events. A popular energy technique is Reiki, which promotes the flow of energy that has been disrupted or blocked by trauma, negativity, stressful emotions, or poor nutrition. There are also breath work therapists who facilitate a breathing process that provides access to repressed emotions stored in our physical bodies. Participants in breath work groups report that they experience healing, both emotionally and physically, at a very deep level.

Many of the natural ways of healing are based on ancient forms of health care. It is interesting to learn and experience these alternative, noninvasive forms of healing. When any of these practices are integrated into our lifestyle, we will feel the positive benefits.

I would like to experience:

My plan:

❖ **We respect, value, embrace, and appreciate ourselves by:**

Taking time for solitude

Removing ourselves from the noise, demands, and whirlwind of activities is a welcome change for most of us. Certainly we realize our importance to others, especially our spouse, children, and grandchildren. However, we are not so important that people will fall apart if we take short times of solitude to renew our energies. Solitude will return us to our center and provide the time to reflect on the special experiences in our lives.

Perhaps you can create a place of solitude where you can go to relax, contemplate, and recharge your emotional batteries. You might want to have a bulletin board with a collection of photos of people you love, favorite activities and places, and positive quotations to read when you are emotionally drained. Reading poetry or inspirational prose, cards from friends, looking at photographs of special times, listening to favorite music, drawing, writing, or meditating are ways to emotionally renew.

Solitude helps us to create the life we want to live, at the depth and breadth we want our life to be. When we are quiet and our heart is open, we can experience insights about ourselves and develop a greater appreciation for life. Taking time for solitude is a way to nourish our souls. It is in solitary moments when we realize that God's love is closer to us than our own heart. In solitude, we are more able to hear the guidance for our life journey and ponder on how we can put God's love into our words and actions. When we are able to combine our quiet moments with the beauty of nature, we connect with the wonder and awe of God's creation. When re-entering our world from the beautiful meadow of solitude, we feel peaceful, appreciative, content, and re-energized.

Self-Esteem

> When I take time for solitude, my experience is:

❖ **We respect, value, embrace, and appreciate ourselves by:**

Discovering and following our passion

Our passion challenge is "Catch the wave!" Passion is fervor, ardor, enthusiasm, and zeal. When we are in our passion mode, we go beyond the limitations that we create in our minds and enter an arena of all possibilities. Our heroes are people who followed their passion. Professional artists reach near perfection in their skills because of their passion. If our spiritual passion is the work we do, we are especially blessed. Passion is part of being fully alive and having vibrant mental, emotional, physical, and spiritual health. Finding our spiritual passion is finding our personal source of joy.

Complacent and apathetic living is an epidemic in our culture. What is often thought to be normal in our society is being an emotional flat line, not sharing deep feelings and not showing excitement. Expressing our excitement and enthusiasm regarding our spiritual passion is contrary to cultural norms. However, we can speculate that a benevolent and life-supporting God intends for us to be totally alive and living our passion, which is rooted in our strengths, interests, and spirituality.

Following our passion does not have to be a *mighty purpose*, although what may start out as a small effort may burgeon into something beyond our expectations. Sharing healthy thoughts and even small acts of kindness are powerful, and we may be able to change a person's despairing situation or outlook for an hour, a day, or a lifetime. Just as we may not know how our accidental ignoring of someone is hurtful to them, we may never know how we impact people with our caring interactions that are rooted in our life passion.

> Reflecting on my spiritual passion:

❖ **We respect, value, embrace, and appreciate ourselves by:**

Going beyond what society considers to be normal

What our society considers *normal* is not necessarily healthy. The mental health of members of our nation is generally poor, evidenced by the verbal, sexual, and physical cruelty that routinely occurs. Our physical health is often compromised because of stress, lack of exercise, and unhealthy nutrition. Expressing emotions is discouraged. Blaming others, rather than taking personal responsibility, is common. We are often dishonest with ourselves and others. Many people acquire possessions and seek pleasure to create security, be stimulated, and fill their emotional emptiness. Too often, spirituality is viewed as an hour in a place of worship, rather than trying to live by spiritual principles every day.

We can go beyond what is considered normal and discover a more meaningful and purposeful life. We can dig deep within ourselves, define our values, and live by them with integrity. We can be more proactive in our health and healing. We can invest our time in worthwhile activities and with interesting people. We can dare to be different in a society that encourages us to follow the crowd. Though we may have actual limitations imposed on us by others, or are limited in some area of our life, we are not self-defeating by putting limitations on ourselves. By revising our limited thinking, we are likely to be surprised at the opportunities and experiences that come into our lives.

Ways that I can move beyond what society views as *normal:*	
Limitations I place on myself:	My *no limit* thinking:

❖ **We respect, value, embrace, and appreciate ourselves by:**

Actualizing our potential

Self-actualizing is becoming what we are capable of becoming. As humans, we are designed to actualize our potential. Our inner voice prompts us to discover who we are, launch ourselves, and become all that we are meant to become. No one can take this journey for us. We are meant to be all that we can be, and leave a legacy that is worthy of the gift of life we have been given. We are honoring, respecting, valuing and appreciating ourselves when we self-actualize and live altruistically, with beauty, grace, and serenity.

There is no end to the journey of self-knowledge, actualization and personal growth. We will:

- ➢ Continue to search
- ➢ Continue to ask questions
- ➢ Continue to live with honesty and integrity
- ➢ Continue to heal
- ➢ Continue to thrive

Reflecting on self-actualizing:

What do you want to say with your life?

Write your epitaph:

I plan to continue to:

❖ **We respect, value, embrace and appreciate ourselves by:**

Living with peace of mind

Peace of mind has been described as the most sought-after emotional state. It does not come from the external world. Peace of mind comes from within ourselves and requires living in harmony with

◄ Self-Esteem

ourselves, others, and God. When we experience peace and joy in our hearts, we live in a different way. Rather than being directed by our desires, fears and ego-behaviors, we let our lives be directed and guided by our higher nature, the spirit within.

Peace of mind comes when we have learned to love, esteem, respect, value, embrace and appreciate ourselves. When our center is peaceful, even though we may be in the midst of personal challenges, we experience peace of mind. When we are at peace with all of our life experiences; when we have no quarrel with anyone; when we are at peace with the part of life that we cannot understand; when we are at peace with the questions that have no answers; when we can say, "All is well," because we know that God is directing our lives and is the source of all blessings, we experience true peace of mind.

Saint Theresa's Prayer: *May today there be peace within. May you trust God that you are exactly where you are meant to be. May you not forget the infinite possibilities that are born of faith. May you use those gifts that you have received and pass on the love that has been given to you. May you be content knowing you are a child of God. Let this presence settle into your bones and allow your soul the freedom to sing, dance, praise, and love. It is there for each and every one of us.*

Does the way I am now thinking bring peace of mind?

Am I behaving in ways that bring me peace of mind?

Does the way I am now feeling bring peace of mind?

Does my spirituality bring peace of mind?

❖ **We respect, value, embrace and appreciate ourselves by:**

Living each day in gratitude

We may experience the blessings of health, creativity, harmony, laughter, music, opportunities, relationships, nature's beauty, joy, and the many miracles that happen. Take time to contemplate on these blessings and be grateful. When we have an active spirituality, we experience gratitude throughout each day. We will speak and pray in gratitude. We become a walking, living, breathing, grateful human being who appreciates the life experience.

I am grateful for:

Chapter 10

Living and Sharing Our Healthy Self-Esteem

There is overwhelming evidence that the higher the level of self-esteem, the more likely one will treat others with respect, kindness, and generosity. People who do not experience self-love have little or no capacity to love others. —Nathaniel Branden

From the moment we decided to start a healing and recovery process, we started changing our thinking patterns and upgrading our behaviors to be more in line with the principles of a harmonious life. We have taken a life-fostering journey, with each step having its rewards. Being a self in the world is challenging. Being the best possible self is even more challenging. When we have healthy, authentic self-esteem, we challenge ourselves to be our personal best. We are meant to be fully functioning and help others to do the same.

We have discovered that our most important journey in life is going inward to discover who we are, what we believe in, how we want to live our life, and how we are going to share ourselves in ways that make a positive difference. We live each day from our inner self and with our total self. We are taking care of ourselves by respecting, valuing, embracing and appreciating our minds, bodies, emotions and spirits. We realize that the core of who we are is love. Our self-talk is mostly positive, and we choose not to expose our minds, eyes, or ears to anything that is violent and evil. Preventing over-extension is important to us, and we do an intervention on ourselves when we recognize that stress is harming our minds, emotions, bodies and spirits. We have discovered that making good choices for ourselves has a positive influence on ourselves, as well as on our families and friends.

We have grown in emotional maturity and arrive at our own conclusions, rather than believing everything that parents, teachers, or society taught us. We experience our feelings rather than avoiding, suppressing, or dulling them with chemicals or activities. Rather than following the directives of a materialistic society, we embrace spiritual principles, which include taking responsibility for ourselves and viewing everyone as equal and valuable. We are now experiencing a more subtle level of experience that is finer, more exquisite; simple but more real and meaningful. Sharing conversations and activities with family and friends is more important than having the latest fashion or the most expensive car. Having lifted the shroud of low self-esteem and changing our views about ourselves, we have upgraded our ways of thinking, and what we believe we are able to do. We are continuing to learn how to live gently, lovingly, kindly, mindfully, peacefully, purposefully, consciously, gracefully, simply, beautifully, soulfully, gratefully, and joyfully. We experience serenity, which is a blessing to the mind, body, emotions, and spirit.

We can now find ourselves among the characteristics of people with authentic self-esteem.

People with high self-esteem:

- Respect, value, embrace, and appreciate themselves
- Think positively and have positive self-talk

- Are honest with themselves and others
- Deal with reality rather than being in denial or creating a false reality
- Take responsibility for their actions rather than blaming others
- Experience new freedoms, such as freedom from harsh and scolding self-talk
- Are less vulnerable to substance or activity addictions
- Do not physically, emotionally or mentally harm others to feel good about themselves
- Are assertive in communicating their needs
- Are less co-dependent
- Experience their emotions and express them appropriately
- Make amends when they have harmed others
- Forgive others and themselves
- Do not harbor resentments
- Respond more to their internal voice, rather than following external cultural directives and trends
- Are self-accepting, compassionate and kind to themselves
- Make healthy choices that positively affect self and others
- Are a good friend to themselves
- Reach out to others in healthy ways
- Take care of themselves mentally, physically, emotionally and spiritually
- Speak and live with integrity
- Treat themselves like they treat their best friend
- Have beliefs and attitudes that are life-fostering
- Live with approval and appreciation of themselves
- Are intent on living fully
- Are confident and stand up for what they believe
- Encourage and want others to succeed
- Are generous with their time, talents and resources
- Are honest with self and others

- Are creative, self-motivating, flexible, and enthusiastic
- Are proactive and plan ahead rather than being reactive
- Believe that mistakes are tools for learning
- Have no need to control and manipulate others
- Celebrate their strengths and achievements in a quiet way
- Are resilient and rebound readily from setbacks and loss
- Feel confident and competent to meet life's challenges
- Are inner-directed and motivated to reach their goals
- Readily meet challenges and are often inspired by them
- Experience and appreciate their successes
- Feel good about themselves because they are living up to their own standards
- Enjoy humor
- Appreciate the miracle and gift of life
- Look for the beauty in all people, places and things
- Live every day with gratitude

Healthy self-esteem results in greater well-being on our mental, physical, emotional and spiritual dimensions of life. A society comprised of high self-esteem people would have many positive qualities. People would be responsible, self-motivated, honest and trustworthy. They would strive to live in harmony with other people, all creatures, and the environment. Our leaders would make decisions that would benefit everyone, rather than a selected few. There would be equality for all in both spoken words and actions. The common goal of individuals would be to create a more peaceful society and world.

> Describe a world where everyone has a high level of authentic self-esteem:

Self-Esteem

Fostering self-esteem in others

A natural outcome of having authentic and healthy self-esteem is motivation to reach out to others in our own self-designed, unique ways, knowing that we are all interconnected. When one person is suffering, we are all suffering. And when one person heals emotionally and learns to love self and others, everyone benefits. Here are some ways to foster self-esteem in others:

- Recognize the importance of self-esteem
- Treat others with respect and see value in every person
- Acknowledge others' strengths and positive qualities
- Empower others by teaching skills
- Focus on abilities rather than disabilities
- Affirm the special talents, gifts, and achievements in others in an honest and sincere way
- Believe that every person has a right to some type of success
- Be a good listener rather than being distracted, interrupting others, or monopolizing the conversation
- Be empathic and try to understand the other person's perspective
- Offer kind and affirming statements
- Encourage others to actualize their dreams and goals
- Be enthusiastic about other people's interests and achievements
- Practice unconditional love
- Recognize your importance to people and be grateful for their love

Fostering self-esteem in children

Whether we are a parent, teacher, day-care provider, grandparent, or any adult who interacts with children, it is crucial that we recognize the importance of self-esteem. To do this, we need to have healthy self-esteem ourselves. Parents are a major influence in fostering self-esteem in their children, which requires consistently attending to children's physical and emotional needs, providing respect, unconditional love, attention, and encouragement; and listening attentively when children are communicating.

Out of all professionals, it is teachers, in schools and preschools, who are the most aware of the importance of self-esteem. If we step into preschool and elementary classrooms, we will hear *esteem-enhancing* statements, such as:

- I like how you think!
- Good job!
- I'm proud of you!
- Your handwriting is awesome!
- We are all glad you are here!
- I like how you are being a good listener!
- Do you need help?
- I want to listen; share with me.
- You are special.
- You can do it!
- Ask for help when you need it.
- It's okay to feel your feelings.
- I like how you are using your quiet voice.
- You are important.
- I like how you are paying attention!
- Be independent.
- You are making this a great day for yourself!
- Have fun learning!

◀ Self-Esteem

When children have their physical and emotional needs met and are treated in ways that foster self-esteem, they are more likely to make good choices and behave appropriately. Fostering children's self-esteem is one of the best ways that adults can prevent aggressive behaviors that are harmful to themselves and others. When self-esteem is fostered in children, they are usually respectful, responsible, and self-motivated.

Unfortunately, many parents struggle with their own low self-esteem. These parents need supportive services from educators and mental health professionals by attending classes for recovery from low self-esteem and to learn effective parenting skills. If parents, who are the most significant people in their children's lives, are willing to learn and practice esteem-enhancing and parenting skills, they will be able to foster self-esteem in their children, in their immediate environment, on a daily basis.

Meeting children's emotional needs enhances self-esteem

Children have emotional needs, which adults are responsible to meet throughout their child and adolescent development. These needs are: 1) to belong; 2) to be someone; 3) to be ourselves; and 4) to go beyond. When we are able to meet our own needs as adults and parents, we are more able to meet the emotional needs of our children. If these needs are met, self-esteem is strengthened. If children experience unmet emotional needs, they are likely to demonstrate more aggressive and other problematic behaviors and develop low self-esteem.

Children will create *survival skills* to meet their own emotional needs if their needs are not met by the people in their environment. However, their decisions are seldom good choices for either themselves or others. Many children respond to family dysfunction by acting aggressively to get attention, or isolate by living in a self-created fantasy world of television or video games. Other children try to become perfect children or overly self-sufficient. When children are emotionally needy, they may choose to comfort themselves by overeating. Emotionally wounded children will often create emotional walls to protect themselves. When belonging needs are not met by parents, adolescents may choose to hang out with friends who use alcohol or drugs; or join a gang, where they are accepted and given a sense of power. When the needs *to be someone* and *to be ourselves* are not met, children will develop feelings of being inferior and inadequate.

Our challenge as parents is to meet these emotional needs not only on an everyday basis, but also when we discipline children. Children's emotional needs are often ignored if parents are reactive and controlling, and punish rather than discipline. Punishment involves being harsh, shaming, and labeling children as bad, which diminishes self-esteem. In contrast, when discipline is used for teaching appropriate behavior, it becomes a learning experience. This way of disciplining children may take some thought and planning, but it is discipline that is sensitive to children's emotional needs and maintains their self-esteem and dignity.

We must start to envision and collectively work together to create a world where all children will have their basic physical, mental, and emotional needs met. Because of having their basic emotional needs met, the stage would be set for every child to have authentic self-esteem, which would be beneficial throughout their lifetime in all areas of their life.

Helping children with developmental stages enhances their self-esteem

Children go through stages of development as researched and authored by Erik Erickson. Successful resolution of these stages fosters self-esteem. In contrast, physical, sexual, or emotional abuse arrests children's development.

The first stage of life involves developing trust with parent/parents or caretakers, who are the major part of the infant's world. Infants gain a sense of trust if they experience consistent care. When they have discomfort, they are made comfortable. When they need attention, the need is met. Talking, cuddling, and playing are all bonding behaviors that help infants learn to trust. If a child's needs are not met consistently, children learn to mistrust and may become overly dependent on their caretaker to feel secure. They may also struggle when meeting new people or having new experiences. Aggression toward the self or others and other acting-out behaviors are not uncommon when the developmental needs of this stage are not met.

During the second and third years of life, children achieve a greater sense of autonomy and discover new physical and mental abilities. Their new accomplishments include developing fine and gross motor skills. When children are offered choices, they develop decision-making skills, feel a sense of positive personal power, and develop a sense of self. If, however, caretakers continually do for children what they are capable of doing for themselves, or are overly critical and focus on their failures, children begin to doubt their abilities to learn and function in the world. These children gain power in their environment by being attention-seeking, stubborn, manipulative, and aggressive, creating vulnerability for later adult personality and relationship difficulties.

When children are four to five years of age, they typically experience a broadening environment. During this stage, it is important that parents provide children the freedom and opportunities to develop in physical, intellectual, and social areas. In this stage, children try new activities, and need assistance, encouragement, and approval. Children who master this stage are not hesitant to try new activities and learning challenges. In contrast, children who are ridiculed and punished when they make natural mistakes, such as spilling their milk or tripping and hurting themselves, develop a sense of shame and guilt.

During the next stage, industry versus inferiority, children go to school, which enlarges their world considerably. Until they are approximately eleven (11) years of age, children in this stage are concerned primarily with the development of academic skills, understanding the purpose of rules, and working and playing cooperatively. The task of industry involves a child's creativity, imagination and interest in how things are made, what things do, and how they work. Children who are allowed to complete tasks and given recognition for finished products feel supported when adults communicate that their efforts, as well as the results of their efforts, are important and worthy. A negative resolution of this stage happens when children are discouraged from engaging in activities that interest them, or constantly criticized about what they do, think, and feel. When adults focus and comment on the mess created or when the child's activities are viewed as unimportant, unnecessary, or wrong, children are discouraged and are likely to view themselves as inadequate and inferior.

The next developmental stage is adolescence, which carries the task of emotionally separating, to some extent, from parents. Peers take a prominent role during this stage, and many adolescents begin dating. Sexuality is often explored during this stage of development. During the stage of adolescence, parents often experience teenagers resisting family rules. Despite teenagers' rebellious behaviors, they usually raise their own children much the same way that they are raised and embrace the family of origin's limits and traditions.

Parents can readily foster the positive resolution of all of the stages that children experience. However, many parents do not realize that their children go through these stages of development. As a result, parents may hinder rather than assist children in achieving a positive resolution to each stage by punishing in a harsh way, expecting children to be perfect, or doing for children what they are capable of doing or learning to do by themselves. When parents make it more difficult for a child to accomplish developmental tasks, self-esteem is adversely affected.

Suggestions for helping children grow in self-esteem

- Never physically, sexually, emotionally, or verbally abuse children, which is always devastating to their emotional and mental development, including self-esteem.
- Learn ways to express your anger in healthy, appropriate, and nonviolent ways.
- Treat all children with respect.
- Never put children in the center of marital conflicts.
- Model the type of behavior you want to see in children. You are a powerful teacher. Children pattern their attitudes, beliefs, values, and behaviors after their parents.
- Recognize your extreme importance in your children's lives. Children depend on you for food, shelter, clothing, physical and emotional security; and unconditional love.
- Parenting is more effective and less difficult when we have parenting skills. Enroll in a parenting class or read reliable information regarding parenting.
- Listen to your children as they express their experiences, successes, difficulties, concerns, anger, and sadness. Though many children have all of the conveniences and the latest toys, school counselors repeatedly hear from students that their parents don't listen to them or spend quality time with them, both of which are necessary for fostering self-esteem. Listening is one of the best esteem-enhancers! We

Living and Sharing Our Healthy Self-Esteem

demonstrate to children that we care and respect them when we are good listeners.
- Eliminate negative verbalizations, such as name-calling and put-downs, or comparing the child unfavorably to others.
- Use your personal adult power as a parent to empower, not control or diminish children.
- Model healthy self-esteem.
- Be honest with children and expect honesty from them. Appreciate and affirm them for being honest.
- If children make mistakes, make it a teachable moment rather than imposing harsh punishment, which has negative emotional effects on children.
- Remember that children do not change their misbehaviors by constantly being told that they are bad.
- Expect appropriate behaviors from children and all adults in the home. We cannot have rules for children that we fail to follow as adults. In families, a limited number of rules should be short, clear, and specific. A rule for one is a rule for all: adults need to follow the same rules that they impose on children. Explain the rules and consequences of the rules. Be consistent. Let children help in developing rules and consequences, when they are at an age where they understand the need and benefits for having rules, like being safe.
- Encourage and celebrate your children's achievements and successes.
- Seek win-win solutions to difficulties. You may want to start family meetings, where everyone is affirmed and involved in a problem-solving process.
- Make requests, not demands of children.
- Apologize to your child when your behavior has been inappropriate, such as being loud and frightening with your anger, irrational in your thinking, or too harsh and punishing.

Self-Esteem

- Solve problems as they arise. Don't let things build up, which often ends up in scary verbal explosions that are frightening for children.
- Model appropriate and effective ways to resolve conflicts.
- Call attention to specific accomplishments, such as nice coloring, neat handwriting, or a great story or poem they have written.
- Teach children to make positive self-statements rather than negative statements about themselves.
- Discourage your children from blaming or criticizing others. Teach them to take responsibility for their choices and actions.
- Teach children how to express feelings appropriately.
- Monitor the content and the time spent watching TV or playing video games. Encourage alternative activities such as exercising, drawing, learning a new skill, being with friends, discussing an educational program, or playing outside.
- Encourage creative play, which develops fine motor, social, and problem-solving skills.
- Challenge your children with increased responsibility that is age-appropriate.
- Communicate love and support through appropriate touch and verbalizations.
- Let children complete everything they can by themselves, without rushing in and doing it for them.
- Let children redeem themselves when they have made a mistake. We, as adults, like to make things right when we have done wrong or offended someone. Likewise, we can help children redeem themselves by saying, "I'm sorry," or having them help to clean up from accidental spills.
- When addressing misbehavior, separate behaviors from the children's personhood. Refrain from verbally attacking,

creating guilt, or shaming them. Children are good people who, at times, make poor choices.
- Express love in appropriate ways.
- Give children choices whenever possible. Choice-making is empowering and lays the groundwork for good decision-making in adolescence and adulthood. Let your children make some of their own mistakes, providing you know that the outcomes will not be physically or emotionally harmful.
- Take children's communications seriously. Though their struggles may seem insignificant to you, they are often very important to them.
- Be respectful of children's private space, unless you have good reason to search for something that is inappropriate, unhealthy, or harmful.
- Encourage independent thinking and learning new skills.
- Make requests, not demands. State expectations in positive ways rather than repeatedly saying "No." Provide reasons for when you need to refuse a request.
- Teach children to learn from their mistakes rather than being a reason to feel bad for long periods of time.
- Affirm your child every day and do it sincerely.
- Model a concern for others and invite them to participate in activities to help others less fortunate.
- Remember that children are a gift to us and need to be treasured and treated with loving care.

Empowering children involves nurturing, encouraging, helping, teaching, listening, sharing, and being consistent and dependable. Empowering children helps them to grow into self-confident, resilient, and responsible adults who have healthy self-esteem.

◄ Self-Esteem

> My plan to foster self-esteem in children:

Note: When a child has special needs, including aggressive behaviors, early intervention is the most effective way to address emotional, behavioral, physical, or mental problems. When interventions are implemented in a timely manner, the amount of emotional trauma is reduced for the child as well as the family.

> **The parenting challenge: The greatest gift that we can give to children is healthy self-esteem.**

Chapter 11

Achieving Emotional Balance

> *The real things haven't changed. It is still best to be honest and truthful; to make the most of what we have; to be happy with simple pleasures; and have courage when things go wrong.*
> —Laura Ingalls Wilder, author

Whether positive or negative, rational or irrational, our emotions are responses to internal or external events and provide us with information. Our thoughts create our feelings, and if we are emotionally balanced, we have fewer difficult emotions that arise because of our irrational thoughts or our over-reactions to situations. We also have fewer emotional upsets because of our inappropriate behaviors.

If we are emotionally balanced, we have a full range of emotions and know how and when to express our feelings appropriately, even in tense and stressful situations. Calm, rational, and emotionally balanced persons are loved, respected, and appreciated. They know that the people who get the most out of life are those people who put the most into life and use their energies in healthy and meaningful ways.

When we were children and were hurt, angry, scared, or we experienced a loss, many of us regained our emotional balance with the help of our parents or caretakers. As we emotionally matured, we were more able to independently recover from setbacks and loss. We could restore our emotional balance unless the event was traumatic and we needed additional emotional support from family, friends, and possibly, from a professional.

Emotional balance gradually develops as we grow older, unless we are using mood-altering chemicals. If we began using alcohol or drugs in adolescence, we may be ego-driven, demanding, and lack self-control well into our adult years. We are likely to be dependent on others, and when we do not receive what we want, we become demanding, in ways that are similar to young children's temper tantrums.

- Mark shares:

    My emotions used to be up and down and I never felt grounded because I was drinking alcohol every day to relax, fill my emptiness and forget about the decisions I needed to make. Drinking worked for a few years, but then it started getting in the way of feeling okay about myself. Now that I am in a Twelve-Step Program and have sobriety, I am no longer an emotional wreck. Much of the drama ended when I stopped drinking. Now I can trust myself and trust my feelings. In Program, they call it emotional sobriety. I have learned to feel and express my feelings in appropriate ways. I feel good about being able to feel all of my emotions but not be controlled by them.

Identifying stressors that contribute to emotional imbalance

Relationships cause stress, as well as insufficient finances, unemployment, or compromised health. We experience stress when we are overwhelmed because of being over-extended. Our work may be stressful. Transitions, such as leaving a relationship, leaving

Achieving Emotional Balance

or starting a job, moving, or other situations that upset our daily routines, also cause stress. Symptoms of stress, which create emotional imbalance, include difficulty concentrating, being negative, misplacing things, worrying, being fearful, forgetting appointments, and having nightmares or panic thoughts.

We can't always change the stress that is created by external events, but we can change the stress that we create for ourselves. If we clearly identify our stressors, we can create a plan to reduce them and achieve greater emotional balance.

Do I create stress for myself…

➢ By talking negatively to myself?
➢ By being over-extended?
➢ By my irrational thinking and beliefs?
➢ By not discarding toxic guilt?
➢ By behaving in ways that harm others?
➢ By not asking for help when I need it?
➢ By suppressing rather than expressing my feelings?
➢ By being disorganized?

What are the key stressors in my home environment?

What are the key stressors in my work environment?

What are the key stressors in my relationship?

Working with our stress is a process that needs to start with **prevention**. By being proactive, we can prevent many situations that cause stress by changing our thoughts and behaviors. However, it's not possible to prevent all situations that cause stress, which means that when we are stressed out, we need to do an *intervention* on ourselves. By consistently implementing both prevention and intervention, we will experience far less self-created stress, which will allow us to deal more effectively with the inevitable stressors that we are likely to experience in life.

Stress Prevention Strategies

- **Modify the amount of time you spend with toxic persons or leave the relationship, if possible.**

- **Remove:**

    - Negative self-talk
    - Negative past learning such as "I am not okay."
    - Negative mind-food such as violence and pornography
    - Irrational, toxic guilt
    - Over-extension: doing too many things for too many people
    - Perfectionism
    - Behaviors that harm self or others

If we are successful in removing or modifying these stressors, our stress is significantly reduced.

- **Other stress prevention strategies**

    - General health and stress resistance is enhanced by eating nutritiously and avoiding alcohol, illegal drugs, and tobacco
    - Maintain both an exercise and relaxation routine

Achieving Emotional Balance

- ✓ Rather than creating unnecessary drama, purposefully live in calmness
- ✓ Refrain from overspending to prevent financial pressures
- ✓ Express your feelings appropriately rather than suppressing them
- ✓ Don't make problems larger than their original size
- ✓ Keep your personal power and refuse to be a doormat to others
- ✓ Simplify your life
- ✓ Work on becoming more organized
- ✓ Keep your self-talk and attitudes positive
- ✓ Count your blessings
- ✓ Use the Serenity Prayer to put things in perspective: *God grant me the serenity to accept the things I cannot change; courage to change the things I can; and wisdom to know the difference.*

Stress Intervention Strategies

- ➢ Laugh and cry. Laughter releases tension. Tears can help cleanse the body of toxic substances
- ➢ Talk out situations that are causing stress with someone you trust
- ➢ Discover ways to recharge your emotional batteries
- ➢ When you feel stress and tension in your body, use calming self-talk and take time to breathe deeply
- ➢ Increase your self-nurturing
- ➢ Reach out and help someone
- ➢ Keep a positive attitude and count your blessings
- ➢ Make good choices for yourself by:
  - ✓ Treating everyone and yourself respectfully
  - ✓ Being with healthy friends or a support group

- ✓ Discarding resentments
- ✓ Being okay with human imperfection and limitations
- ✓ Creating a vision for yourself

Releasing stress to promote emotional balance

We can release stress by **increasing** our physical activity in non-competitive ways:

- Aerobic exercise
- Walking, jogging, rollerblading, swimming, and other individual, noncompetitive physical activities

Or, we can reduce our stress by **decreasing** our physical activity:

- Meditating
- Listening to music
- Being quiet and reflective
- Visualizing
- Doing biofeedback
- Having a massage

> Achieving emotional balance is an everyday goal. Today, what have I done for myself…
>
> Mentally?
> Emotionally?
> Physically?
> Spiritually?
> What have I done to enhance my relationship/s?
>
> If we have positive answers for all of these areas, we are doing well in our efforts to achieve emotional balance. We will experience being loved, being able to love others, and living a life that is meaningful and purposeful.

When we are emotionally balanced, we are self-confident and are able to self-advocate when people trample on our rights. We have wholesome principles that guide our life and we have healthy relationships. Because we are emotionally balanced, we can usually be calm in the midst of chaos and are good problem-solvers. We work well with others, and people seek us out and enjoy being with us. All of these behaviors indicate a high level of self-esteem.

Chapter 12

Visualizations, Affirmations, and Expressions of Gratitude

Believe in perfect health, prosperity, peace, wealth, and divine guidance. Claim that the healing presence in your subconscious is flowing through you as harmony, health, peace, joy and abundance.
—Joseph Murphy, author

Research supports the following premises:

1: We are mental, physical, emotional, and spiritual beings, and our natural state is to be healthy on all of these levels. One of the basic principles of holistic or *whole-being* health is that being healthy is optimal functioning on our mental, physical, emotional, and spiritual dimensions of being. The body, mind, and emotions are not separate from each other. Rather, they are interrelated, and each is affected by and influences the other. Our bodies are designed to be healthy, but chronic negative mental and emotional states cause enormous stress on the physical body and are underlying factors in disease.

2: Humans are designed to be self-healing. There are natural healing activities accessible to all. The following are activities that promote and maintain our health and help us to heal when we experience illness:

- Exercising and also relaxing routinely
- Affirming and appreciating our bodies
- Appreciating the perfect intelligence we have in every cell, organ, and body
- Sharing our feelings with someone we trust and who listens to us, with the intention of understanding our experience
- Spiritually connecting to a power greater than ourselves
- Having a positive attitude and self-talk
- Praying
- Accepting and loving ourselves.
- Having healthy, authentic self-esteem
- Participating in loving relationships
- Actively going through the emotional grieving process when we experience loss
- Being in contact with nature
- Involving ourselves in music, art, literature, and theatre
- Enjoying body massage, or being touched, or touching in healthy ways
- Doing activities that are purposeful and provide meaning in our lives
- Enjoying healthy sexuality
- Helping and fostering growth in others
- Using our minds to visualize health

3: Imagery is a natural function of the human mind and can be used to help prevent illness and promote healing. Visualizing is doing consciously what we already do unconsciously. Visualizing is seeing pictures in our minds, much like when we are reading a novel. We imagine the characters, what they are doing, and the setting they are in. Therefore, we *already know* how to visualize. We routinely form mental pictures or images in our minds when we are thinking about a specific project or goal, when we pray or meditate, or how we want to perform when playing sports, teaching a class, or doing other types of activities. Mental imagery involves using our minds in an aware manner, to promote and maintain health, to help our body to heal, or to help us achieve our goals.

Mental imagery is also called creative imagery, creative visualization, mental training, guided imagery, or guided meditation. Everything that exists starts with a thought. That is why Dr. Albert Einstein stated that "Imagination is more important than knowledge." All of our experiences are the direct result of our thoughts, which involve our mental images and beliefs. What we experience in life, what we do, who we know, where we go, and what decisions we make begin with the thoughts and images that we have in our minds.

Mental imagery and our physical bodies

Our physical bodies reflect what is transpiring within us on the mental, spiritual, and emotional dimensions (Gawain, 2002, Hay, 1999, Schultz, 1998). Though our bodies communicate with us, we often do not listen. When we fail to listen, our bodies will manifest in minor or major illness. Studies have shown that many of our current illnesses begin at an emotional level, and subsequently manifest at the physical level. Emmett Miller states, "Deep healing recognizes that whenever there is any significant health issue, mind, body, emotion and spirit are *always* involved" (Miller, 1997).

Imagery is similar to meditation and prayer. All of these reflective techniques have been used by people for centuries to relax, to promote good health, to create what one desires, and to help others through thoughts and prayers. Visualizing, meditating, and praying are ways of using our minds in a creative and healthy way and are not practices used exclusively by any specific religion.

Guided imagery exercise

This guided visualization exercise is focused on affirming and healing our physical body. It is not to be used as a replacement for medical advice and treatment. It is meant to be a self-help exercise to help prevent illness and relieve minor pain. It can be used along with medical treatments that you might be receiving. This imagery is followed by a series of positive affirmations and gratitude statements, which places us in the highest levels of energy, where there is less physical and emotional disease.

This program has a spiritual focus, and there are many names used for God, such as Universal Intelligence, Higher Power, or a Power Greater than ourselves. Please use a word that fits your individual beliefs.

Now we will begin.

Find a comfortable position, either sitting in a chair or lying down. Close your eyes if that is comfortable for you. We have no other place to be except here, in these moments, with ourselves. Breathe deeply. As you inhale, image positive energy coming into your body and filling every part of your body with warmth and light. Then exhale, and image all negativity, stress, and any burdens that you are carrying, whether you are aware of them or not, leaving your body. We will do this several times so that we become totally relaxed.

Again breathe deeply, and as you inhale, image positive energy coming into your body, filling every part of your body with warmth and light. Then exhale, and image all negativity and stress leaving your body.

Again breathe deeply, and as you inhale image positive energy coming into your body, filling every part of your body with warmth and light. Then exhale, and image all negativity, stress, and any burdens that you are carrying, whether you are aware of them or not, leaving your mind, emotions, and your body.

Now feel yourself so relaxed that your body is floating down through the chair or bed, or imagine your body being as relaxed as a child's rag doll. Repeat several times, "I am very relaxed. I am very relaxed. I am very relaxed." Feel the quietness within you. Stay with this quietness, serenity, and peace.

Now, slowly and gently, image a white light, a spiritual light, God's light, or a light from the Universal Intelligence – whatever name you would prefer to call it that is most meaningful to you, and is a power greater than yourself. This light is pure and life-fostering. This light is healing and has perfect intelligence. The light can help to heal parts of your body that are struggling with pain, being out of balance or out of place. The light wants only the best for you. This white light is perfect love and when invited is a healing power for you.

Image this white light around you and within you, breathing with it for a few moments. Then invite the light to come into your body and begin healing, restoring, renewing, and balancing all aspects of being: the body, the mind, emotions, and spirit. Breathe deeply and relax.

Form an image in your mind of the light going to your head. Your brain is located close to the sensory organs that provide vision, hearing, balance, and smell and is so miraculously complex that it is beyond understanding. Send love and appreciation to the 100 billion neurons in your brain that each has perfect intelligence and works in so many ways for your benefit. Image the light as keeping your mind and memory clear, and your thoughts positive.

Now form an image in your mind of the light going to your eyes and strengthening the cells in your eyes, so that each eye cell has perfect health. See your eyes very relaxed and functioning perfectly. The pressures within your eyes are normal. For a moment, ponder on the miracle of sight. Encourage your eyes to be healthy and affirm your eyes for the marvelous gift they are in your life. Out of love and respect to your eyes, resolve to view only that which is healthy. Take a moment to bathe your eyes with your appreciation.

See the light moving to all of the other intricate organs in the head—your ears, nasal passages, mouth, and throat. The light focuses and heals any condition that may need the light's attention. We know that the light has perfect intelligence, as does each and every cell of our body and all of our organs. We know that the body wants to be vibrantly healthy and very often heals itself. We know that we can help the body heal on its own if we maintain positive thoughts and attitudes. We know that the body functions and heals best when we make conscious efforts to stay relaxed.

Now totally relax once again. Take a deep breath. Affirm all of your body, mind, emotions, and spirit and say, in your mind or out loud, "I am very relaxed!"

Now visualize the light moving to your internal body. Image your major organs as being relaxed, working efficiently without strain, working with love and in your best interest; working happily and perfectly. Image your organs being very efficient when they work within your relaxed body – they are master artists at what they are designed to do and work willingly and diligently. Image your sexual organs as healthy. Visualize all of your organs that keep you internally clean and balanced, as working effectively and diligently, but effortlessly. Image perfect breast health. Visualize your complex endocrine system working for you, with joy.

We know that loving and taking care of ourselves, through good nutrition, exercise, forgiving those we need to forgive, letting go of old anger and resentments; and having positive thoughts and excitement for life are our responsibilities and are effective ways to help our bodies be healthy. Now… image all of your organs working cooperatively with one another, helping one another, and being encouraging to one another. All of your organs welcome the healing light.

The light then travels to your arms, wrists, and hands. For a moment, think about all the experiences that have enriched your life and have enabled you to enrich the lives of others because of the mobility and versatility of your arms, wrists, and hands. You have nurtured children and comforted those in pain. You have created beauty by tending a garden, painting a landscape, playing music on an instrument, making a Valentine, or planting a tree. You have carried a newborn child, taught a skill, folded the laundry, paid your bills, cleaned, cooked, repaired things broken—all of these things have been able to happen because of the capabilities of your arms, wrists, and hands. In your mind, acknowledge how your arms, wrists, and hands are so important in your life. Send love and appreciation to your arms, wrists, and hands and tell them how valuable they are to you, in doing so many activities for yourself and others.

The light then moves to your legs, ankles, and feet, which are vital in being mobile. Imagine these parts of your body as relaxed, free from pain, and working perfectly. Just thinking about moving your toe will cause the brain to send a message that results in your toe moving almost instantaneously as you have the thought. Ponder on the miracle of this phenomenon. Reflect on the many places you have been, the many things you have done, that have required your body to move in so many different ways. Send appreciation and love to your legs, ankles, and feet.

Image your arteries and veins being totally clear and your circulation being perfect. Image your immune system as very strong and protecting you. In your mind, see your digestive system as calm, relaxed, enjoying and pleased at what you eat and drink and functioning without strain and working perfectly. See in your mind, all of your digestive system as being joyful. Image your strong bones and healthy joints, free of anything that would encumber movement or create pain.

Take a few moments to think about the miracle of your whole body, on how your body provides you with so many opportunities of seeing, hearing, doing tasks, moving, creating, writing, walking, and so many other kinds of activities. Image the light healing, comforting, or repairing any areas that need healing attention, and believe that your healing is happening in this very moment.

Now send love, appreciation, and encouragement to all parts of your body. All parts of your body are important, beautiful, and miraculous. All medications prescribed by the best doctors for you are working perfectly. All parts of your body are valued and appreciated. If there is any pain, view the pain as passing through and not staying in your body. The pain is moving out of your body, with the help of your belief and your images. All parts of your body are relaxed and feel the healing that the light provides. Say an affirmation that you are radiantly healthy—"I am radiantly healthy."

Imagine all of your body systems working perfectly. The bodily process of taking in and letting go flows smoothly, and there is no strain. The taking-in process and the letting-go process are also working in your mental, emotional, and spiritual life. You are able to discern what to take in and what to let go of, such as old resentments, anger, hurts, negative thinking, and things you were taught that are not true or life-fostering. The body is so often a metaphor of our emotional life, so be willing to love yourself more; and forgive and let go of anything that would stop a smooth flow of energy in your body.

Repeat these words: "The thoughts that I think help me to heal. Healing is happening on all levels of my being—the physical, mental, emotional, and spiritual. My healing is perfect. Yes, I believe this to be so."

Conclusion of imagery

Be grateful for all of the blessings you are receiving in your life, including the ability to participate in your own health and healing. Ask the light to heal you all through the night during sleep, and all through the day during activity. Be still and know that all is well in your world, that all relationships and all experiences are both meaningful and sacred. Learn to live with greater serenity, harmony, and balance. Be at peace. (Rogne, C. *One Canoe, Many Paddles – Healing and Living Our Spirit.* Outskirts Press, 2010).

Use this guided imagery often. Make additions that apply directly to your health concerns. Remember, guided imagery is a natural function of our minds and can be used to enhance our physical, mental, emotional, and spiritual health.

A guided imagery for peace in our world

In your thoughts, imagine a world where there is physical and emotional safety, healthy nurturing, respect, and equality for everyone. In this world, all children have food, shelter, and safety. They are educated by caring adults and also taught the ways of kindness and honesty, rather than the ways of war and violence. In this world, all children will not be afraid and will fall asleep at night in complete peace. Together, we will make this a reality.

> *That is the ultimate point of creative visualization—to make every moment of our lives a moment of wondrous creation, in which we are just naturally choosing the best, the most beautiful, the most fulfilling lives we can imagine.* —Shakti Gawain

Affirmations

Positive affirmations are present moment, active statements. The following affirmations will enhance healing on the mental, emotional, physical, and spiritual dimensions of being:

- I turn my will and life over to God.
- I pray to be a clear channel that responds to people in peace, serenity, and wisdom.
- I am as amazing as I let myself be.
- I choose thoughts that support and nourish me.
- I am healthy and joyful.
- I enjoy learning.
- I am enough, I have enough resources to sustain myself, and I do enough.
- I reach out to others in healthy ways.
- I am glad to be alive and that I can experience life fully.
- I am creating life just the way I want it.
- I love my miraculous mind!
- Energy flows freely through me.
- I am healing in all areas of mind, body, and spirit.
- I am creative and use my creativity to make things better for myself and others.

Self-Esteem

- I allow higher wisdom to direct and guide my way.
- The universe nurtures and supports me at all times and in all places.
- Living one day at a time brings me peace, joy, and serenity.
- I am receiving healing in this very moment.
- The healing light removes any discomfort in my body.
- I have an inner peace that cannot be disturbed by outside events or situations.
- I feel healthy, prosperous, and excited about life.
- I trust my inner truth and God's guidance.
- I have enough energy to do all the things I want to do.
- I am graceful, beautiful, and loving.
- I am loved and cherished by many people.
- I feel nurtured by myself and others.
- I feel the presence of Higher Power in my life.
- I love who I am and what I do.
- I see miracles happening with myself and others.
- I am healing in mind, body, spirit, and emotions.
- I am able to relax or sleep peacefully.
- I love my body, mind, emotions, and spirit.

Grateful Statements

- I am grateful for my family and friends.
- I am grateful for my open mind, which welcomes new learning.
- I am grateful that I have a caring and loving heart and am able to speak kind words to all of the people I meet each day.
- I am grateful for my feelings of joy, wonder, love, fulfillment, peace, and serenity.
- I am grateful for my talents and the opportunity to share them with others.

Visualizations, Affirmations, and Expressions of Gratitude

- I am grateful for life.
- I am grateful for the blessing of work.
- I am grateful for new experiences.
- I am grateful for God's guidance and answered prayers.
- I am grateful for the miracles I see and appreciate.
- I am grateful for God doing for me what I could not do for myself.
- I am grateful for the emotional healing that God has given to me, so that I am free from negative thinking, resentments, harmful addictions, fear, anxiety, depression, and selfishness.
- I am grateful for my creative mind and the opportunities to use my mind for good purposes and helping others.
- I am grateful for my healthy body.
- I am grateful that God created me wondrously and marvelously!
- I know that I live only by God's grace.
- I know that God's love is closer than my heart and beyond my understanding.

Epilogue

Recovering from low self-esteem takes courage. Meeting all of the challenges that life presents to us requires courage as well. I would like to share the prayer I wrote about courage.

Grant Me the Courage

To accept, embrace, and appreciate myself
To move beyond my self-imposed limitations
To walk through my fears
To say "no" when it's important to refuse
To participate in my own healing and choose life
To believe in myself
To make amends when I have harmed others
To stand up for rightness and goodness
To say "yes" to life
To reach out to others in healthy ways
To trust my inner truth and my growth process
To arrive at my own conclusions
To advocate for the change of inequities and injustices
To receive from others as well as being generous in giving to others
To be different when the world demands conformity
And most of all, the courage to love in an oftentimes unloving and unkind world—to love myself, others, and to love God, with all of my heart, mind, and soul.

References

A.A. World Services, Inc., New York, NY.

Gawain, S. *Creative Visualization—Use the Power of Your Imagination to Create What You Want in Your Life.* Nataraj Publishing, 2002.

Hay, L. *You Can Heal Your Life.* Hay House, 1999.

Miller, E. *Deep Healing.* Hay House, 1997.

Rogne, C. *Anger and Guilt – Our Foes and Friends.* Outskirts Press, 2011.

Rogne, C. *Who's Controlling You? Who Are You Controlling? – Strategies for Change.* Outskirts Press, 2010.

Rogne, C. *One Canoe, Many Paddles – Healing and Living Our Spirit.* Outskirts Press, 2010.

Schultz, M. L. *Awakening Intuition: Using Your Mind-Body Network for Insight and Healing.* Three Rivers Press, 1998.

Carol Rogne Empowerment Resources
website address: carolrogne.com

Also By Carol Rogne

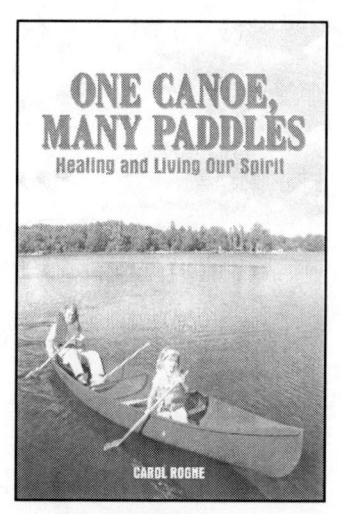

One Canoe, Many Paddles

A crucial step in our healing involves removing harmful false beliefs, resentments, and ways of thinking that are negative, fear-based, and limited.

Having removed what is sabotaging our lives, we can then create a life with more positive ways of thinking, behaving and relating. This will enable us to move closer to optimal health on all levels of our being: the mental, emotional, spiritual and physical.

One Canoe, Many Paddles – Healing and Living Our Spirit, describes the personal growth journey and offers life skills that enhance our effectiveness and reduce stress.

The book delves into many spiritual principles, including the Twelve Step Program, and suggests ways of expressing, celebrating, and living our spirit with gratitude.

Learn more at:
www.outskirtspress.com/onecanoemanypaddles

Also By Carol Rogne

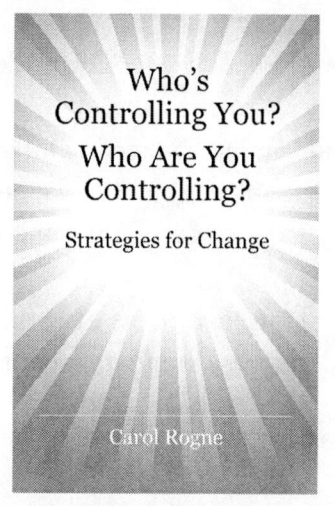

Who's Controlling You? Who Are You Controlling? - Strategies for Change

Considered one of the best books ever written on power used to control others, this book defines emotional and mental control as interpersonal violence that creates trauma in the emotional lives of adults and children.

You will be empowered by the topics:
- The many ways that power is used to control others.
- Characteristics of controllers and the people they control.
- Strategies for positive change:
    - Protecting ourselves from emotional abuse
    - Confronting, rather than enabling controllers' manipulative, life-diminishing tactics.
    - Re-claiming and designing our life based on personal choices, values, beliefs and goals.
    - Surrendering controlling behaviors if we are

controlling others.
- Restoring relationships damaged by controlling behaviors.

We can recover from the emotional devastation of being controlled. Our empowerment journey will result in becoming a healthy person and parent and end with a message to share, especially with our next generation, that we all have certain rights, among them being, "life, liberty, and the pursuit of happiness."

Learn more at:
www.outskirtspress.com/whoiscontrollingyou

Also By Carol Rogne

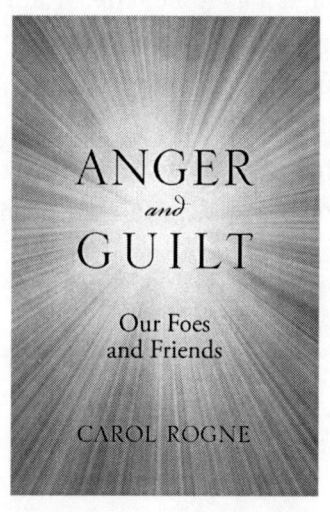

Anger and Guilt

Both anger and guilt can be experienced as enemies or friends. While anger is abusive when it is expressed aggressively, it is a legitimate and appropriate response to emotional, mental, physical, or sexual abuse. Healthy anger is also a stage in the grieving process. The guilt that we generate by our irrational thinking is life diminishing. In contrast, healthy guilt prompts us to change dysfunctional behaviors and make amends when our actions have hurt others.

Topics presented in this practical, easy-to-read book include:
- Anger and guilt are controlling behaviors that can be confronted assertively.
- Anger and guilt alert us to areas in our life that need changing.
- Anger and guilt strategies can transform our lives and enhance our relationships.

By growing in awareness, we can discard the belief that anger and guilt are enemies that sabotage our life. Rather, we can appreciate these emotions as supportive friends who provide us with valuable information to help us navigate more effectively through life.

Learn more at: www.outskirtspress.com/ angerandguiltourfriendsorfoes

CPSIA information can be obtained at www.ICGtesting.com
Printed in the USA
LVOW082306160912

299000LV00001B/16/P

9 781432 794019